BEAUTIFUL BUTTERFLY
HEALING FROM MOLESTATION AND DEPRESSION

ANISKHA D. JOHNSON

Largo, MD

© Copyright 2020 Aniskha Johnson

All rights reserved under the international copyright law. No part of this book may be reproduced or transmitted in any form or by any means, electronic or mechanical, including photocopying, recording, or by any information storage and retrieval system, without the express, written permission of the publisher or the author. The exception is reviewers, who may quote brief passages in a review.

ISBN 9781562293918

Christian Living Books, Inc.
P. O. Box 7584
Largo, MD 20792
christianlivingbooks.com
We bring your dreams to fruition.

Scriptures taken from the Holy Bible, New International Version®, NIV®. Copyright © 1973, 1978, 1984, 2011 by Biblica, Inc.® Used by permission of Zondervan. All rights reserved worldwide.

DEDICATION

I dedicate this book to my mom who asked God, "I did my best to always make sure I protected her, why did this happen to my daughter?" My mom prayed every day, asking God to restore everything that was taken away from me as a child. This book is her answered prayer. God has restored my life way more than she could ever imagine.

ENDORSEMENT

This book draws out your emotions. As I read, I felt Aniskha's pain and distress. She took me on her journey. It's incredible how someone can endure such a great magnitude of pain yet overcome. It is a clear message that you can conquer anything with the help and strength of God. This book is astonishing. It will influence and inspire you. It shows the importance of having a good support system. Aniskha overcame this horrific experience with the help of her husband, relatives, and friends.

–Sherique Dill
Author, Inspirational Writer, and Writing Coach

CONTENTS

Foreword IX
Introduction 1

LARVA STAGE

    Chapter 1 – Unworthy of My Father's Love 3

    Chapter 2 – Betrayal of Trust 7

    Chapter 3 – Only Bad Things Can Happen to Me 17

    Chapter 4 – Wanting to Be Normal 27

PUPA STAGE

    Chapter 5 – Trying to Build Relationships 33

    Chapter 6 – The Bride with All Her Baggage 41

    Chapter 7 – True Happiness or Very Dark Days? 49

    Chapter 8 – It Will Not Get Any Better 53

    Chapter 9 – There's Only One Way Out 67

    Chapter 10 – God Was Always There 75

ADULT: BUTTERFLY STAGE

    Chapter 11 – Bad Thoughts vs. Good Thoughts 83

    Chapter 12 – Opening the Vault 91

    Chapter 13 – Freedom through Christ 107

Acknowledgments 117
About the Author 121

FOREWORD

It is a special privilege to write the foreword for this book. It is straight-forward and well-written, describing the shame and pain experienced by many victims of child sexual and physical abuse.

The Adverse Childhood Experiences (ACE) studies show that early sexual child abuse produces deep shame that is lodged in the unconscious life of the person. This relational trauma and its accompanying dysregulation block the child from flourishing and enjoying life. It impedes the child's ability to grieve, express deep feelings of commitment and to appreciate simple experiences of joy. In essence, it really destroys the child's ability to thrive. We now know that early childhood abuse does not only produce psychological and emotional issues in adult life (e.g. depression), but also physiological issues like diabetes and hypertension. The harsh reality is that the child is forced into the enslavement of victimhood that runs throughout his or her life. Our research has shown that many persons with high ACE scores end up with destroyed lives, committing various acts of violence and also suffering from physical illnesses.

This book is special because Mrs. Johnson bravely describes her own journey through child sexual abuse. She willingly faces the shame and describes how it haunted her as she moved through different phases of her life, often creating a psychological wall between her and those around her. She describes this inner pain as horrible and sometimes intolerable. However, the good news is she was willing to face the challenge of her painful experience by working with a competent therapist. As a result, she was able to heal from the deep wound of abuse and move on into a life of meaningful fulfillment and service to others.

Finally, Mrs. Johnson has shown how her deep Christian faith has allowed her to forgive her perpetrators and move into the experience of joy, forgiveness, and love. I highly recommend this book as a very special contribution to the Adverse Childhood Experiences literature and how we can snatch victory from the jaws of victimhood and defeat.

–David Allen, M.D., M.P.H.

INTRODUCTION

I recall as far back as my first day in kindergarten feeling excited—no crying. I was just ready to learn and experience the world. I had no idea that one day, my passion and innocence would quickly be overshadowed by new emotions I wasn't equipped to handle.

One of my classmates was getting all the recognition. So at the tender age of four, I tried to analyze the difference between us. What did she have that I didn't? She had a lot more hair than I did. Fact of the matter is girls with short hair didn't seem to be loved by the outside world, so I wished for longer hair, wanting to be like her.

In my little mind, I thought my teacher was paying more attention to her. However, in retrospect, that was only my perception. These feelings of low self-esteem changed my entire perspective on life. I wasn't the excited little girl anymore. In fact, I didn't even want to be Aniskha, I longed to be someone else. I wanted to feel loved and be told I was pretty.

Those negative encounters in my life from a young child to an adult led me to accept the lie that only bad things could happen to me. However, my life is evidence that if you have experienced the same thing, you can be restored. Even as an adult, God can reconstruct your life, heal your pain and brokenness and transform you from a larva into a beautiful, free butterfly.

Chapter 1
....

UNWORTHY OF MY FATHER'S LOVE

At home, my grandparents, mother, uncle, aunts, and older cousins loved me. I had all the attention because I was the only child in the house. Surrounded by all this love, how could peer pressure cause me not to feel loved?

We expect to be loved by our families and why shouldn't we? We resemble them and our characters are shaped by the family environment we live in. However, at certain stages in our lives, we also crave the acceptance of those outside our families. For some of us, this desire can be so strong and overwhelming, it causes us to succumb to peer pressure.

Peer pressure comes in various forms. But I was influenced by unspoken peer pressure. My peers did not tell me to do anything directly but I saw them engaging in certain activities, and I felt the need to do the same.

At a tender age, I was a deep thinker. I would sit, watch, and analyze situations. This is not always good because like me, you can end up having preconceived thoughts that are not correct.

Throughout kindergarten and primary school, I watched my peers. I observed how they looked, behaved, and interacted. I also saw how people responded to them.

Mirror, Mirror

I noticed the girls with fairer skin and long hair got all the attention. I assumed these girls were better than me because of their appearances. All these negative thoughts flowed into my mind, and I believed them.

I was born to a teenage mother. She was a single parent receiving minimal assistance from my father. I love my mom greatly, and I know she loves me. I also loved my father whom I didn't interact with often.

> *Negative thoughts flowed into my mind, and I believed them.*

My mother always told me I didn't like to embrace anyone during my toddler years. She said I would cry continuously. She also said no matter how long or far in between I didn't see my dad, when I did, I would go to him with open arms and no tears.

The love I had for my dad was unexplainable. However, I processed in my little mind that I wasn't pretty enough for him either because I didn't have long hair like the other girls who received all the attention at school.

The unspoken peer pressure at school dominated my thoughts and intruded on my family life. My self-confidence and self-esteem deteriorated steadily.

Like me, many children face the same battle every day in our schools and homes. To combat this and help them understand their true value in God's eyes, it is important to teach and emphasize the following memory verse and others from Scripture:

> I praise you because I am fearfully and wonderfully made; your works are wonderful, I know that full well. (Psalm 139:14)

The exciting world I wanted to embrace was overshadowed by sadness and the need to be accepted. I went through a fantasy stage. I pretended something existed that didn't just to fit in. I would tell my peers I was with my dad for the weekend, and we spent a lot of time together. Sometimes, I would go so far as to say my mom and dad were together. I even fantasized about being scolded by my father. I became a shy, quiet girl who craved attention but gave a false impression to those around me. I also became a compulsive liar.

Add to the List

In the first grade, my teacher told my mother I needed speech therapy. She said I didn't pronounce my words correctly. These therapy classes were being offered at the school weekly. The classes didn't last long, and I am not sure to this day why, but I never completed them.

This was another issue added to my list. I had short hair, received little attention and now, I couldn't speak well. Consequently, my shyness soared to another level. I was very conscious of how I pronounced my words and feared being laughed at by my peers. Asking questions in class was a no-no. Although I needed answers, I would say nothing because I feared drawing attention to my speech impediment and being laughed at.

> I concluded I wasn't worthy of my dad's love.

Once again, being a deep thinker at a tender age, I concluded I wasn't worthy of my dad's love. I could see why he didn't visit me much. I took full responsibility and blamed myself for what was happening.

All the doubts and insecurities that crept into my mind at that age affected me straight into adulthood.

Chapter 2

BETRAYAL OF TRUST

The fifth grade was an unusual year for me in school. My pain and insecurity were heightened to another level—one a child should not be able to express or even comprehend.

In primary school, I was a good student. Track and field was something I did well. Although classified as shy, I was also a part of the choir and recorder group. Still, I felt I wasn't worthy to have a father, and I was unhappy most of the time. To avoid reality, I kept myself busy doing several extracurricular activities.

I participated in the long and high jumps, as well as the 100-meter and 200-meter races because of my speed. At nine, I was tall compared to my classmates, and I had long legs, which made track and field easy for me. My physical education teacher recognized my potential, so he asked me to compete in an inter-school primary sports event. I practiced three times a week after school with other classmates.

My physical education teacher was entertaining, energetic, and charismatic. We felt comfortable with him because he was not a disciplinarian; he was easy-going. One day, he gave me an affectionate nickname that changed my world; it brought a sense of happiness to my life. I felt special because I was the only one with that nickname. This was it. He identified what I lacked. He made me feel beautiful and that is exactly what I desired. I needed to know someone outside my family loved me, not just anybody but a male who could fulfill the role of a father.

Out of My Way

The nickname along with his smiles made me feel comfortable being around him. Every day, I made sure he looked at me. I would deliberately pass him in the corridor or on the field during lunchtime. I would go out of my way to run into him just to hear that nickname and to see his smile. I also loved getting a pat on the shoulder. These interactions drew me closer and closer to him. My physical education teacher was occupying the void left by my dad. He showed me the attention I craved.

Practices became important, so I made sure I didn't miss them. I love track and field, but I also loved the attention and being embraced by this male figure who gave the impression he could be a dad.

One day, I went equipped for practice, but only a few children turned up. He called me into the physical education room. While I was there, the unimaginable happened: he hugged me. Something felt strange, but I wasn't sure what it was. I was uncomfortable, and I wondered if being hugged by my dad would feel that way. Why did this hug feel so strange? I got hugs at home, and I always felt love from the warm embrace but this one seemed different. Yet, I thought, "It's fine. I have to get familiar with this."

Another practice came around, and I received another hug in the same setting; no one was around. Again, I felt uneasy, confused, and worried. I wasn't sure if this was what I wanted. It just didn't feel right. I didn't want to go to his classroom anymore. I liked the nickname and smiles, but I didn't want the hugs.

The Favorite

Time passed, and I was still his favorite being called by the nickname. But I noticed when others were around, I only received smiles and a pat on the shoulder. After realizing this, I would bypass his room. However, if he signaled me to come in, I would go because he was my teacher, an authority figure. I still wanted to stay respectful, and I didn't want him to stop making me feel special.

> *I didn't want him to stop making me feel special.*

Then came the day I would never forget. He ordered me into the room again. This time he gave me the unusual hug and touched me inappropriately. Instantly, I knew it was not right. But he told me it was our little secret, and I would always be his little miss. He said other adults won't accept this behavior and would be angry if I spoke about it. I believed him. I did not want anyone to be angry with me, and I needed to feel his love, so I kept what he said was our "little secret."

Even though the touches were inappropriate and displeasing, after a while, it became the norm. Shyness took control of me. I was too timid to say no, so I accepted it as ordinary. Some days, I went home in pain and most days, I tried to accept that this was a part of being loved by a father figure.

My teacher betrayed my trust. I depended on him at first because he made me feel special and loved, but he exploited my vulnerability.

You may think it is foolish, and you might ask, "Why would you allow someone to make you feel uncomfortable repeatedly?" The answer is that as a child, I was searching for love but from the wrong person. I had hopes that one day, this would feel natural. I can tell you now it never felt normal, no matter how much I wanted it to. I felt animosity toward him, but I didn't know how to stop the violations. I had no idea what to do.

At age ten, I entered the sixth grade, which was an interesting year for most students. But, for me, things got worse. One day, at the inter-school sports competition, I finished a race, but I didn't do well. Actually, I came last. I cried uncontrollably. My teacher, seeing my vulnerable condition came to "soothe" me. He told me to tag along with him to pick up lunch for the team.

The Detour

We were heading toward Kentucky Fried Chicken to pick up lunch when he made a detour to a remote beach. I sat in the car shaking with fear because I knew something was wrong. I wanted to ask him where we were going, but I was too afraid to speak. I worried that if I showed my emotions he would get angry.

I noticed he had brought a towel with him as we walked deep into an area surrounded by trees. I was petrified and wanted to run. But I didn't. Why didn't I run? That is a painful question I asked myself. I was ten years old. I didn't know where I was, and I was afraid he might catch me if I ran.

He held my hands, and we talked about the track event, as well as how I felt. He tried to reassure me I would do better in my next race. It was almost like a father-daughter connection, and he showed me distinct stuff on the beach. This is one time I didn't want his affectionate smile or words.

He found a spot that was not visible to anyone passing on the road. There, he spread out the blanket, and we both lay down. I was asthmatic as a child and to this day, I don't know how I lay there without having an asthma attack.

He moved from inappropriate touches to kissing and fondling to attempted rape. I cried as he removed my clothes. "Stop!" I sobbed. This was the first time I had built up the courage to tell him to stop. He tried to console and persuade me to believe it would be okay and that I was special to him. He said, "It won't take long, but you need to relax and trust me." Only this time, the affectionate nickname and his attempted reassurance were not sufficient for me to relax.

My heart was racing fast. I wanted to scream for my mom. I wanted to scream for help. I desperately needed someone to come and rescue me. Just as he was about to rape me, he said, "Don't be afraid; this is new for you, but it will be a wonderful feeling."

He's Always on Time

I begged him through tears, "Please, stop! I want to go home. Please, let me go home." Just then, a helicopter flew over us. He stopped, fixed his clothes, then mine, and pretended he was showing me the helicopter.

You might say, "What a coincidence." I claimed it as God's perfect timing. God saved me from that horrific, unbearable experience. I felt terrible and traumatized. The helicopter must have broken his will because he bundled up his belongings, and we took off after that.

Shockingly, we didn't head straight back; we still

> *God saved me from that horrific, unbearable experience.*

went to get the food. I cried the entire time. I was in disbelief; I wasn't sure what had just transpired, but I knew what he did was wrong, and I never wanted to encounter that again.

No One Noticed

As I sit and write this book, I remember he did not show any remorse for what he did. He gave no explanations for his actions. I was horrified, and I cried constantly, I heard nothing he said. I was still crying when we got back to the sports center. No one suspected anything because I was crying when I left so when I came back crying nothing seemed strange to anyone. I couldn't participate in any more events that day; I felt sick. I had a terrible headache. I sat in the shade for the rest of the day in a daze. Just like that, my childhood innocence was swept away.

Upon arriving home that day, my mom did not notice anything wrong because of my quiet nature. And besides,

I didn't tell anyone in my family about these incidents because I promised my teacher this was "our little secret."

While watching television with my mom one day, we saw a scene about an adult hurting a child. My mom exclaimed emotionally, "Let me know if anybody ever hurts you. I will deal with them!" When she made this statement, my mind recalled all the things my teacher did. I was thinking, "Yes, I want someone to hurt him because he hurt me." Yet, I didn't want him to be mad with me because he made me feel so special.

My character as a child was to show love and compassion. I didn't like confrontation or to see others get hurt. So even though the thought came to my mind that I wanted him to be hurt, I really didn't mean it. When my mom made that remark, I pledged never to tell her about my teacher. I didn't want him to get hurt or for my mother to go to prison.

The hugs and inappropriate touches ended because I was graduating from primary school. I was glad to leave this school, hoping I would never have to see him again and all those bad memories would fade away.

Summer of that year was interesting. I went on being a child but those bad experiences influenced my thoughts and mind. Really, they controlled my entire life. I felt I was missing something and even though I wanted the inappropriate touches to end, I believed I needed them.

One day, I began experimenting on myself and did the same things my teacher did. Sometimes I would use an object or just my hands. This went on for most of that summer and many years later into my early teenage years. The more I did it, the more I disliked my teacher. I couldn't control this urge; it was close to an addiction. However, one day, after years of masturbation, I stopped. This was another act of how awesome God is and how He delivered me.

Chapter 3

ONLY BAD THINGS CAN HAPPEN TO ME

The results were out. I took entrance exams for three high schools, and I passed all three. Attending a school that had good sporting facilities was important to me because I loved sports. My mom had her mind set on another school because the Christian beliefs and values lined up with hers. Sadly, I was not impressed by the school she selected because their sporting facilities were not great.

Even though the school was not my first preference, I was delighted to be entering high school. It came with a lot of nervousness because I didn't know what to expect. My first semester was all right. It definitely was a relief not to have to deal with my previous physical education teacher.

Doubts and insecurity continued to control my mind. I remained timid and fearful of speaking because I felt the children would laugh at how I pronounced some of my words. Plus, I felt they could look at me and detect someone had molested me. The blame game started, and

I felt I had made bad choices. Thoughts of regret plagued my mind: "I should have stopped track and field; that would have ended all the practices I had to attend." "I hate myself for going with him to pick up the lunch that day." "I should have obeyed my mom and stayed at the Sports Center." "I should have known a teacher could not replace my dad."

He Followed Me

Low self-esteem kept me away from most of the children because I felt the majority of them were better than me, and they didn't make dumb choices as I did. I was sure if they figured out my secret they would scorn and reject me. I had set up a mental and emotional wall that separated me from my peers.

You see, I had left the school where the abusive physical education teacher was, but he followed me to my new school in my mind, emotions, and in totality. He still had power over me. I carried the burdens of guilt and shame.

> *Thoughts of regret plagued my mind.*

I became close to two girls whom I admired. One of them I wished I had her personality. She could stand up for herself and no one would take advantage of her. I said to myself, "If I was like her then my teacher from primary school would not have done what he did." Today, I know better because some adults have a way of exploiting children. Regardless of personality type, abuse can happen to any child.

My other friend had attended the school for a longer period, and she was familiar with its operations, so she kept me informed. Despite what I was secretly hiding and feeling, we had a lot of laughter together.

Not Again!

By the second semester, darkness closed in on me again. A boy from a higher grade teased me regularly. Every time he saw me, he would sing out, "Thick lips!" My self-esteem was already low and here I was again dealing with another issue that affected my self-value. I didn't know how much more I could take. I would smile when he sang out, "thick lips!" but every time he said those words, I felt as if I was being stabbed with a knife.

Those stabs cut through my mind, soul, and heart. I wanted to run and hide somewhere and cry, but I had to pretend to be brave. I had to act as if those words were not hurting me. I believed these bad things happened because I was ugly. I said to myself, "I must be the ugliest student here." The teasing caused me to develop a bad habit of trying to hide my lips hoping they wouldn't be noticed, but he still continued to tease me.

Today, unconsciously, I still hide my lips. My husband makes me aware of it and I stop, but it happens again. I don't do it because I feel ugly or ashamed of my lips now, but the trauma is still there. Every day, I continue to work toward breaking this habit. Bullying has a long-term effect on people's self-esteem. I don't support it. Mental and emotional abuse can be as detrimental as physical abuse.

Hurt People Hurt

The teasing caused me to become vengeful; I teased those who were obese. Why would you tease someone when you know how teasing affects you? I wanted others to feel exactly how I felt: hurt, ugly, and unhappy. It was my way of distributing the pain, as well as masking my hurt and insecurities.

A student in my class also started to torment me. He would touch me inappropriately when no one was watching, mostly under the desk. How could this be happening? I thought when I exited primary school, I had left all the bad things behind, but I was wrong. Why didn't I speak up and tell him no? Why didn't I tell my teacher? I was so trapped in fear and traumatized, I could not utter a word. I still believed what my primary school teacher told me: adults just won't understand. This student was also older than me and the way he looked at me was very intimidating.

> *Bullying has a long-term effect on people's self-esteem.*

One day, we were having classes outside. There was a hill at the far back corner of the school; it was a secluded spot. Sometimes we would have classes there on the benches. The male student decided to sit next to me. Why didn't I get up and sit somewhere else? I would ask myself. I was very afraid of being exposed and embarrassed or being classified as a bad girl. Besides, people might think it was all lies. What proof did I have?

That same day, he bothered me again under the table. This time, my face must have shown pain and discomfort because, at the end of the class, my teacher asked me if everything was okay. A thought ran through my mind that this was the time to speak up. But again, timidity and fear took charge. I thought, "If I say I am not feeling well, she could send me to the nurse. It would just appear as if I am ill and no further questions will be asked." This was challenging for me because I didn't want to go to the nurse's office, and I didn't want to get anyone in trouble. I dismissed all those thoughts, nodded quietly, and said, "I am okay."

A Teacher's Heart

I don't think my teacher believed my answer, but she accepted it. However, she referred me to the guidance department, which sparked a relationship with my guidance counselor.

Counselors are trained professionals who have a way of asking children indirect questions to get answers. But as I mentioned before, I was a deep thinker, and I knew where she was going with her questions. I knew she felt something wasn't right with me, and I was afraid to tell her the truth about my classmate. To escape the situation with my classmate, I told her what happened in primary school.

The results of that conversation were unexpected. She wanted to get my mother involved. I was petrified and bewildered. I had vowed to never tell her my secret. I didn't want my mother to know. I wasn't sure if she would be angry with me for not telling her, if she would be disappointed or punish me because I left the Sports Center that day with my teacher. I was also afraid she might hurt the teacher.

My guidance counselor arranged the meeting with my mom. I sat there quietly while my guidance counselor did all the talking. I trembled and my head hurt. What would the backlash be? I knew my mom loved me, and she always did her best to protect me but once she was told, I wasn't sure if she would be upset, hurt or angry.

On our way home, she didn't ask me any questions. We did not talk about it. The only thing she told me was I needed to tell my dad. This was difficult for me because I was only 11 years old.

Unmet Expectation

I called my dad out of obedience and asked him if he could stop by the house because I had something to tell him. He agreed, and he came after work. With fear in my voice, I told him what happened. I could not read his feelings, but I would never forget the words he said, "You need to forgive the teacher and then move on. I have to leave, but I will come to see you another day."

Now, as an adult who is more spiritually mature, I understand the importance of forgiveness; however, at eleven years old, I had no clue. I was devastated because I expected a different reaction from him. I expected, at least, this one time I would get a hug or feel loved by him. He did the opposite. Was he on my side or my teacher's side? When I thought about it, I reminded myself that my father did not love me, and I was ugly. Why did I think his reaction would be different? On that day, I vowed to never discuss my issues with my parents again.

I was angry with my parents. I was angry with my mom because she told me to tell my father. I was angry she didn't just hold me and tell me she loved me, and she was sorry that it happened. I was angry with my dad because I was expecting him to show his anger toward the teacher. I wanted him to hold me and assure me everything would be okay.

I was totally convinced now that I should expect nothing good to happen to me. If it did, it had to be a mistake.

Later in my adulthood, my mom explained she thought the best way to protect me was not to let anyone know. She wanted to keep me from shame and people harassing me. All those years, I thought she never tried to protect me, but she was doing so the best way she knew how.

This must have been painful for my mother to endure. I can't imagine having to deal with that as a parent. I thank the Lord for keeping her strong through those difficult times. Even though I was angry growing up, I always knew deep down inside she loved me very much; I am her world, pride, and joy. Now I am older and have my own children, I understand she did what she felt was right. She prayed for me and kept me covered. I am now at peace knowing she did her best.

An Empty Void

I went back to school the following day void of any feelings with a pretentious smile on my face. But all I wanted to do was cry all day. I continued to have encounters with my classmate along with the other student who continuously teased me about my lips.

> *I had vowed to never tell her my secret.*

At eleven, I developed strategies that helped me to become numb when I encountered these challenges. Whenever I was being touched, I blocked any uncomfortable feeling or pain from my memory. I would become numb to my surroundings. This was my survival tactic through seventh grade.

As I reflect on the past and different situations, I know despite what I was going through, God was with me every step of the way. He held me in His arms. During those times, most days in class I was in a daze. I was there physically, but I could not focus long enough to listen to my teachers. I also didn't have the energy to learn. Surprisingly, I made it through seventh grade. It could only have been God who carried me through.

I dreaded returning to school the following school year in eighth grade to face my classmate and the teasing. To my surprise, he did not return. I was happy and relieved. I don't know why he didn't come back, but it was a joyous occasion for me. However, the teasing about my lips did not end. One student teased me until his final year in high school, which was three years later.

> *I developed strategies that helped me to become numb.*

In eighth grade, I became interested in track and field again. I wanted to join a track club. I spoke with my mom, but she wasn't excited about the idea. She told me if my dad was involved then I could do it.

I Was So Excited

I spoke to him about it, and he agreed to allow me to workout with him in the mornings. It still wasn't confirmed that I could join the track club, but I was glad just to be with him. He came for me early in the mornings when he would go to exercise.

My dad was always into fitness and lifting weights. I was so excited because I felt we had something in common, and he would probably love and accept me even if I wasn't beautiful to him. But after three occasions, he stood me up. I was crushed and angry with myself. I felt irresponsible for believing that this was the beginning of a relationship when I knew deep inside, he didn't love me, and it was probably worse after I told him about my former teacher. He was probably disgusted looking at me. I definitely knew I was disgusted when I looked at myself. These were my insecure thoughts. From that day, I vowed not to ask him to help me with anything again or even speak to him.

I didn't do well not speaking to him. The few times he came to visit, I was excited to see him and still hoped to be daddy's princess. He allowed me to visit him a few times and play with my younger siblings. I loved them so much. I loved my little sister, but I was jealous because I felt she was daddy's princess, and I was out of the picture.

Chapter 4
....

WANTING TO BE NORMAL

As the years went on, I tried to lock all those bad memories far away. My life seemed normal, but something was missing. Have you ever encountered this feeling before? I was waking up every morning, not experiencing the joy and happiness I should have had because there was a missing part of the puzzle.

In senior high school, most of the girls had boyfriends. I didn't want to appear to be "out of the norm," so I figured I would get a boyfriend too. However, relationships didn't last long for me. Deep down inside, I thought they were gross and disgusting but to show a good face and be a part of the crowd, I got involved. I hated it so much that even something as simple as holding a boy's hand made me uncomfortable.

During my teenage years, I became close to a dear friend from church—Sarah. How we became close was one of God's plans for both of our lives because she became my pillar of strength during our adult lives. I didn't like her at first because she barely spoke to me and others in the church. She was fair-skinned and had long, pretty hair. I believed she received more of the attention at the time because she was pretty and confident.

One day, Sarah's mom asked my mom if I could attend a sleepover she was having for her. I was excited to go because my mom never allowed me to sleep out. Nevertheless, because she knew the family and their strong Christian values, she accepted the invitation. It was a very awkward feeling for me as I was the only one there from our church. All the other friends were in her class from school. They spoke fluently and were confident about themselves. This intimidated me because I was not confident.

> *This intimidated me because I was not confident.*

She Has It All

My admiration for Sarah was strong. She had a dad in the home who loved her. She was pretty, had long hair, and spoke eloquently. I said to myself, "Wow, she has it all!"

I thank God for directing her mom to invite me because this sparked a friendship between us. I realized later that she was a great person. We had similarities: she was just as shy as I was despite being pretty and getting more attention. One day, I shared my experience in primary school with her. Even though we were teenagers she was very caring, and I also appreciated that. Today, we are still close friends.

My mother made sure I stayed active in the church. I attended Sunday school regularly, and I was a part of Awana and discipleship classes. Around the age of 14, I became close to one of the Awana leaders. At times, even though I tried to block all my memories, dealing with the trauma was strenuous for me. I didn't know who I was. I felt dirty most days and some days, I wanted to cry all day or be held by someone who could comprehend what I was going through.

One day at Awana, I had a yearning to talk to someone and hear the words, "It's okay." I built up the courage to talk to this male Awana leader. Why did I reach out to a male and not a female? Subconsciously, I still craved that father figure in my life. This counselor loved working with us, and I felt he had a caring heart. That day, he assured me everything would be okay. I needed to hear that.

> I always felt I had to lie about who I was.

I was frustrated by all the thoughts Satan had placed in my mind. I felt I needed those inappropriate touches to survive and to feel loved but deep down, I knew it was wrong. I always felt I had to lie about who I was. I wanted to portray that I was this girl who wasn't afraid. I did mischievous things and continued bullying others by calling them bad names. I hid behind my sense of humor.

Even though I was older, I was still holding on to that nine-year-old girl who was confused, hurt, and traumatized. I tried to handle the situation as best I could but the healing wasn't there. I needed healing, I needed help.

What Could Have Been

Being a teenager wasn't exciting. All I could fantasize about was being a child again with no trauma attached. What would my life have been like as a teenager if I hadn't encountered such trauma? A battle was raging in my mind. Satan was trying to lead me astray, but God was there fighting for me.

This leader and I became close. I labeled him as my brother. Calling him my big brother was the closest to having a father figure. I didn't mind having a big brother during all that went on because I felt he would have protected me. I compared him to my teacher who said I was special and that is why we had our little secret that brought me so much pain.

My big brother at Awana assured me I was special. He required nothing from me. He was genuine and also promised me God loved me. I compared him to my dad. However, he was different. He made time for me and checked in on me. Could this be it? Did I finally find someone who could love me and fill this void?

He never mistreated me even when I felt I deserved it. And that confused me. My mind was so distorted from the molestation that I felt men should use me. A part of me didn't desire this. Yet, another part said it was what I deserved.

My big brother set up counseling sessions for me. The first time I visited, I was extremely nervous. I had no idea what to expect. Many thoughts rushed through my mind and clouded my thoughts. I wondered if the counselor would understand or if she would ask me why I didn't speak up. I was scared and shaking.

My Fault

I went to a few more counseling sessions at which the counselor kept saying it wasn't my fault. But I was so tired of hearing that. Deep down inside I believed everything that was going on in my life was my fault.

Counseling only focused on the molestation, but at the core, I struggled with low self-esteem and feelings of rejection by my father whom I was certain didn't love me. I wasn't honest when I went to counseling, so it didn't work, and I gave up.

> *Deep down inside I believed everything was my fault.*

I graduated from high school by the strength and grace of God. Most of my classmates were sad to go but this was one of the happiest days of my life. I was eager to leave my horrible high school life behind. I didn't fit in with the other children. Inside, I wanted to be a leader and a student who got top grades, popularity, and acceptance. But I was far from that.

Thoughts of what happened clouded my mind, and I was afraid it would happen again. Fear continued to paralyze me and keep me from speaking out. I didn't interact well. I only wanted to turn back the hands of time and be that innocent child again.

I could not perform at my full capacity in high school because of all the hurt, shame, and guilt I carried with me. But God was with me. I graduated from high school and got accepted to the College of the Bahamas, which is called the University of the Bahamas today.

Chapter 5

TRYING TO BUILD RELATIONSHIPS

I met my husband at 18. We were a part of the same marching band. By this time, I had learned how to deal with my past. I locked away all those feelings and memories in a vault. I gave up on trying to become "daddy's girl." At the time, that method seemed to work, but it was not healthy. I wouldn't advise anyone to do this.

On our first date, we walked in the mall. He held out his hand to hold mine, but I pulled away with disgust. When we spoke about our first date a few years later, he said at that moment, he thought, "This is a crazy girl." I guess he loved my craziness because he married me, and we are still together.

As we grew in our relationship, he required more from me. The first time we kissed, it was a disaster. It was a disaster for him because I didn't know how to kiss, and it was a disaster for me because it made me feel filthy. I was confused about my feelings because I knew I had buried those memories deep inside my mind. I was a new person. I shouldn't have felt that way.

We tried kissing again and again. It eventually got better for him, but I still felt dirty and those hidden memories popped up one by one. On the outside, I was a calm, smiling young lady but in my mind, I was fighting to ignore how much my heart was aching. I was trying to disregard the memories. This frustrated me because I wanted to feel normal. But kissing made me feel abnormal. Being in an intimate relationship unleashed the memories of my past. And once again, that negative thought raised its ugly head: "Nothing good will happen for me."

> "Nothing good will happen for me."

I eventually wanted out of the relationship. I had two boyfriends previously but the relationships never lasted long. I walked away from both. Eventually, I broke up with my boyfriend (my now husband) but this one was different; it didn't go the way I planned. We got back into a relationship.

A Burden Lifted

Now, I was under pressure to tell him about my past. I wanted him to understand why I was acting this way. I developed the courage I needed, and I told him. It's amazing how I called it my past, but it was front and center in my present and was getting ready to disrupt my future. After I told him, the burden was lifted because now, I was hoping he could understand why I didn't like hugs, kisses or even holding hands.

We dated for seven years before we got married. During the dating period, I still struggled with being touched by him. It irked me when he called me pretty. I would get really agitated when any male told me I was pretty for that matter. That word just always brought back horrible memories. I would instantaneously have a recollection of my teacher. I carried the hate for that word from a child to an adult. The only difference was as an adult, I would give a fake smile and say thanks.

Although I told Perry (my husband) what happened, he still didn't understand why I felt that way with him because he wasn't my teacher or classmate. This was a frustrating point in our relationship. Sometimes, I felt telling him about my past was a mistake. I didn't know how to explain my emotions. I also felt guilty that I couldn't really be who he wanted me to be because I really loved him.

> I didn't know how to explain my emotions.

Can't You See?

This caused me to be angry. I was angry with myself and my parents. I was doubtful. I wasn't sure if my mom really loved me. How could my mom love me if she didn't see the hurt I was carrying all those years? I was angry with my father and didn't respect him. When adults who knew my father reminded me of how much I look liked him, I would get very angry or even sick. I didn't want anything to do with him at all.

In my early twenties, I had just started living. I had practiced locking my memories far away for a number of years. I would numb myself from any physical interactions with my boyfriend at that time. Some days were overwhelming, but they were far and few. I found a way to hide my tears. When those days appeared, I would feel a little sick to the stomach but eventually, I would be okay. So I started accepting this as my new normal. I neither felt it would get any better nor worse. I believed once I could hide the hurt and pain I was feeling, everything would be fine.

I pursued modeling to see if it would build my self-esteem. I always made sure I looked nice, so I could feel pretty. I tried many things to feel beautiful but every day when I looked in the mirror, all I saw was ugliness, scars, hurt, and thick lips. I saw a little girl who just wanted to be "daddy's girl." You cannot replace self-love, self-confidence, and pride with materialism. I can testify to that.

> *I started accepting this as my new normal.*

True beauty comes from within. No matter how well-groomed we are on the outside, it's our inner selves that matter the most.

The Ugly Truth

Many days, I looked astonishing on the outside, but I still felt ugly and filthy on the inside.

> Your beauty should not come from outward adornment, such as elaborate hairstyles and the wearing of gold jewelry or fine clothes. Rather, it should be that of your inner self, the unfading beauty of a gentle and quiet spirit, which is of great worth in God's sight. (1 Peter 3:3-4)

In this scripture, Peter is talking to wives but this advice can be applied to all females. I'm not saying we shouldn't look nice and be comfortable with our outward appearances, but I'm saying healing must come from within.

I had two other friends I became close to. I met Amber at the College of the Bahamas (well, she claims we knew each other before; it's always funny because I don't remember this). Even though I eventually dropped out of college because I had no will power to focus, our friendship continued, and we are still friends today. I met Kim at one of my first jobs during college.

Even though we were close, I wasn't totally open with them, but they knew what happened. On the other hand, I was totally transparent with Sarah. By this time, she was off to college. We didn't talk much because the advanced technology like Facebook and WhatsApp didn't exist at the time. But when we communicated, I would talk to her about my feelings. I allowed myself to be vulnerable with her. She was different. It's almost as if God gave her the discernment to know if I was lying about the way I truly felt.

You've Got to Deal with It

She always encouraged me to deal with my feelings because if I didn't, life would get worse. But I always dismissed her suggestions. She wanted me to attend counseling, but I told her I wouldn't. I had already tried several times with different counselors, and it made no sense. She disagreed; she felt I was never honest with the counselor or myself and that is why it didn't work. Truth is I didn't care what she said. I knew I wasn't going back. I would continue to suppress my feelings until they faded away.

> *I was never honest with the counselor or myself.*

I was petrified by men, especially older men. If I walked past them, I would be nervous. I didn't want to make any eye contact or speak with them.

As a young adult, I felt so embarrassed because my friends were relaxed when having conversations with men, but I was always nervous. I felt I had a sign only visible to men saying, "My body is yours; you can use me."

I was a master of pretending. I told lies to hide how I felt about people, situations, environments or conversations. I believed that conversations about sex were disgusting. Why would anyone like sex? I pretended I was fine with these conversations or I would do my best to avoid them. When I heard the word "sex," it was as if I was stabbed in the chest. That word brought pain to my soul and flashbacks of dreadful memories every time.

While my female friends were having conversations about sex, I would fight not to think about the past. They confused me because they were so enthusiastic about it. But I wondered, "Why don't they understand sex destroys lives?"

I enjoyed going out with my friends to social events. I wanted to be like them having fun and finding pleasure in life. However, even though I enjoyed it, emptiness and fear were always there. During these events, I was very afraid to be alone. When men approached, I would cringe. Inside, I would cry, shake, and pray that they didn't touch me. I felt the minute they put their hands on me or flirted with me, I would vomit all over them.

I loved to dance and most of the time, I would get lost on the dance floor to hide and avoid any conversations. I would also hear Sarah's voice in my head nagging me to deal with the issues before they got worse. I would have a battle going on in my head because I didn't want to hear her voice. I preferred to silence her inside my mind. We didn't get to talk regularly, so her voice did eventually fade away.

Chapter 6

THE BRIDE WITH ALL HER BAGGAGE

In 2001, my husband and I got engaged. I was excited but the emptiness and unsolved issues were still right there. Marriage was the right thing to do, and I desired it. However, the challenges I encountered as a child created many debilitating emotions.

I wasn't sure if our marriage would work, but I knew my husband loved me, and he was the only guy who made me feel comfortable. So that was a plus for me. We set the date for one year later. Plans for the wedding took place. I asked my uncle (who has passed now, may his soul rest in peace) if he would give me away. He declined because my father was still living.

I was devastated by his response because I didn't want my father to give me away. Frustrated and upset, I said to my mother, "No one will give me away. If my uncle won't do it. I will just walk alone." My mother did not agree. She told me he was still my father, and he deserves respect despite my feelings for him.

My mom knew how I felt about my dad, but she never allowed me to disrespect him. She also never spoke ill of him in my presence. She always reminded me of this scripture verse:

> Honor your father and your mother, so that you may live long in the land the Lord your God is giving you. (Exodus 20:12)

As I got older, I reflected on that memory verse. My mother and I talked about it. It didn't say we should only honor our parents when we feel they deserve it. But in spite of our feelings toward them, we should respect them. I obeyed my mother's advice and agreed to let my father give me away at the wedding. After making this vow, I was sad and troubled. I wanted to obey and grant my mom her wish, but I knew I shouldn't walk down the aisle with my dad without expressing my feelings to him.

Closure—Sort Of

I had to make a choice to talk to him for the first time about these deep-rooted issues to bring closure. I called him and asked him if we could meet for lunch. He agreed, and we met. I told him about the wedding and my mom's suggestion. I said I wanted my uncle to give me away instead of him because he didn't know my fiancé or me well enough to fulfill the role of a father and give me away at my wedding.

My dad had never met my fiancé. I felt there should have been a relationship so that when the pastor asked, "Who gives this woman away?" he could happily and comfortably say, "I do." I also built up the courage and asked him, "Why didn't you defend me when I told you what happened in primary school?" I told him how that hurt me and left a long-term scar. He admitted he was wrong and being young, he didn't know how to accept it or what to do. This hurt even more. I was confused as to why he didn't talk to someone and ask what to do instead of just ignoring it. I didn't accept his apology. However, I hid the pain and pretended everything was okay.

I was 25 years old and July 27, 2002 was one of the happiest days for me. Perry and I got married and all our friends and family were present to share in this joyous occasion. But I didn't realize that my happiest day would lead to depressing years in the future. I was in love but never once did I imagine my past was about to interfere with our marriage. After the glitz and glamour of the wedding came the honeymoon and then reality as a wife.

Not Living Up

Our first few years of marriage were awful. I didn't live up to the wishes and desires of my husband, and he didn't live up to my expectations. About three years into our marriage, he admitted he thought once we got married, intimacy wouldn't have been an issue. I could not fulfill his desires because my mind and body rejected the thought of intimacy; it made me cringe. It felt disgusting, and I was angry with God for making this an important factor in marriage. Even kissing had become worse for me. Many nights, I cried myself to sleep.

As the years progressed, it got more difficult. Now, I wasn't only feeling sick, but I was also having horrible nightmares. In most of those bad dreams, I was being raped or someone was attempting to rape me. Someone always had me pinned down, and I would fight to get away. I would have nightmares in which I was running from a gang of men or just one man. On waking up, I would be exhausted. It felt as if my whole body was wet and full of dirt. I would take a hot bath hoping this would make me feel clean. Did this work? No, because I was clean on the outside but emotionally and mentally damaged. It was something a physical bath could not cure. I was fighting deep, spiritual strongholds embedded from my childhood.

Harder to Ignore

Intimacy was very sickening. I would make excuses to avoid it. This put a strain on our marriage. The relationship we had when we were dating changed. The emptiness I was still feeling inside was becoming harder and harder to ignore. I questioned why I got married when I knew I could not fulfill my husband's desires.

Our relationship was a perfect picture for those on the outside but disfigured at home. My past kept our marriage from operating the way God intended. Hurt and guilt were tearing me up inside and created a desperate desire in me to feel loved. Though married, my nine-year-old mind was in control. Why couldn't my husband just fulfill what I was longing for from my dad?

We no longer communicated much because he was upset about our intimate life and felt depressed. He didn't understand what I felt, and I didn't understand his feelings. He consumed his time playing dominoes every evening, and I was home feeling lonely. I went back to college to complete my bachelor's degree during this period. On those lonely evenings, I would try to focus on completing my schoolwork.

The Wedge

At work, we communicated with our coworkers in the other islands through Yahoo Messenger. A friend and I would also chat through Yahoo Messenger while at work. I had known him for a few years prior to my marriage. Our conversations were so refreshing they filled the void that existed at home. However, nothing was easing the pain from my past that was stored away in my heart and mind.

Our conversations got intense. We had lunch dates, but I was always the quiet one. I didn't like to be around men that much, but it was relaxing for me because it was not much of a face-to-face relationship: we mostly sent messages to each other. Satan was trying to destroy my marriage. He was trying to deceive me by distracting me from my husband. He was trying to destroy me as an individual but despite it all, God was in control.

Two Birds

I became pregnant with my first son. It wasn't a planned pregnancy, but I knew it was all God's planning. This pregnancy allowed me to step away from this friendship that was about to ruin my marriage.

The announcement of my pregnancy was exciting news for my family but not for me. My uncle was ill, and I never got to tell him I was pregnant as he died a week after I found out. It devastated me. Why was this happening? My uncle promised he would fight cancer, but he didn't. I was angry with him. And I was also mad that I was pregnant because I wasn't ready to be a mother. That nagging lie came back to haunt me, and I said to myself, "Nothing good will happen for me so just live with it."

Three weeks before my oldest son was born, my grandmother passed away. She died from a broken heart six months after she lost her only son—my uncle. I was ready to give birth soon and everyone around me wanted me to stay calm. How was that possible when I lost two family members who were instrumental in my life? From birth, they contributed to my well-being and remained in my life until death.

I was pregnant and had lost two of my loved ones. During that time, I was also in the process of completing my bachelor's degree. It was another act of God's love and His fight for me. I completed my final exam to achieve my degree two days before my oldest son was born.

Chapter 7

TRUE HAPPINESS OR VERY DARK DAYS?

March 9, 2005, God blessed me and my husband with a son. That was genuine happiness for me. However, it only lasted until I got home with my bundle of joy who cried non-stop.

About three months after my son was born, I made a doctor's appointment and was diagnosed with postpartum depression. I wasn't familiar with the feeling at first. I had read about it, but I didn't feel it could happen to me.

The doctor scheduled a visit for me to see a psychiatrist. I thought, "Not again, I am not going for any counseling because they don't care about me as an individual; it's just a job to them." However, I respected my doctor, so I went.

The psychiatrist asked a few annoying questions, gave me some medicine, and scheduled my next appointment. I went about three times then I stopped. It was just too frustrating for me to sit there and listen to someone tell me what I should do when he didn't really know me.

My days were getting darker, but I found some joy in my son's eyes. My dear friend Sarah came home and visited my son. I could not be honest with her at this time because I didn't want to hear her repeat those words, "Nish, you need to do counseling. It will only work if you are honest about your feelings." I pretended everything was going well. But I wanted to just cry on her shoulder. I wanted to tell her about the frequent nightmares and how awful intimacy was for me. I knew she had an idea that something wasn't right; she always had a discerning spirit. I think she respected what I wanted and preferred me to discuss my issues with her if I wanted to.

Overwhelmed

I became pregnant with my second son two years after I had my first. He arrived on February 13, 2008. Another happy occasion but now, I had a toddler and baby to deal with while I struggled with all the hurt inside.

My life became an exhausting routine. There were tensions with my husband. I was taking care of two young children, going to work and at the same time, trying to make church a priority. After I had my first son, I rededicated my life to Christ.

I knew that my mom was a Christian. She made sure I attended church and taught me Christian values. I knew she prayed for me, and I wanted the same for my kids.

When I became an adult, I got caught up in worldly things, but I never departed from the values my mom taught me. I always felt guilty when I did wrong. Despite where I went on Saturday night or what time I got home early Sunday morning, I didn't miss church on Sundays. I knew I had to follow the principles my mother taught me. The conviction of knowing right from wrong and what God expected saved me from making bad choices many times. I wanted to make sure I followed God's Word:

> *I always felt guilty when I did wrong.*

> Train up a child the way he should go and when he is old, he will not depart from it.
> (Proverbs 22:6)

I had to be certain when my children grew older, they would have the spiritual foundation needed to make good decisions.

Parenting issues became another burden on our marriage. Both of us had different parenting styles. I could not get my husband to understand me or for us to be in one accord with parenting; it divided us. The intimate issues we were having in our relationship made it worse because he was frustrated with me, so he never agreed with anything I said.

Chronic Affliction

Time was moving fast. Sadness and emptiness were taking up more space than any joy or happiness I might have felt. I was getting exhausted. I had chronic illnesses and was in the doctor's office at least once a month with some complaint. My throat used to feel as if it was closing in, and it was hard for me to swallow. It was as if I had a lump in my throat that would cause me to choke. My doctor referred me to a specialist; nothing was found to be wrong. I experienced chest pains and also felt I couldn't breathe. I was referred to a specialist again, but nothing was wrong. I had scans done because of the migraines I was having that made me feel faintish, but everything came back fine.

I wasn't enjoying life. Negative thoughts were all I knew even though it didn't look that way to those around me. I knew I had to fight for my life and there were still things I needed to do for my family, but my mind was telling me to just let go. I wanted to let my marriage go so my husband and I wouldn't always have to be frustrated. But I would constantly hear a small, weak voice saying, "No, you must fight." That being said, there was another loud voice assuring me I was born for nothing good. Every day, I was in a chronic mental battle.

Chapter 8

IT WILL NOT GET ANY BETTER

I felt as if I was always being attacked by men, not only physically but verbally as well, which is just as serious. As I mentioned before, I never learned how to interact with older men. I was afraid they wanted one thing from me—to abuse my body. I didn't speak with confidence around them, and I was afraid to be alone with them.

One day at my job, a coworker said he admired my legs. I had such a bad feeling when he said that. I didn't know how to respond. I felt he was going to attack me. I got nervous and started sweating, but I pretended to be fine. When he left my office, I wanted to burst out crying, but I had to compose myself.

I was angry because once again, I didn't stand up for myself. In my mind, I asked, "Do you want to be molested again?" I engaged in self-talk and said, "I think you like that because you're not saying anything; you're sitting there like a dummy." Time went on and this same co-worker continued to make inappropriate comments to me. As usual, I said and did nothing.

Flashback

On another occasion, I went to his office to take a letter. He approached me as if he wanted to kiss me and hold me down. His stare was frightening and unforgettable. I got an instant flashback of my teacher when he was holding me down on the secluded beach. I was so afraid that I froze. I was too weak to move. That day, I cried and cried in my car asking God, "Why me? Do I have a sign on my head that says, 'easy target'?"

I composed myself because I was getting close to home. I felt sick and by the time I got home, I had a terrible migraine. I wanted to crawl into bed in a fetal position to cry and sleep. But, with two young kids that was impossible. I didn't tell my husband what happened. I told him I didn't feel well, and I also had a migraine, but he thought it was my familiar excuse to avoid him. I didn't have the strength to argue or explain, so I let it be.

> *I was angry because once again, I didn't stand up for myself.*

I struggled at work from that day on. I tried my best to shun this man, but it was difficult in the small company. I wasn't verbally harassed every day, but I felt stupid and angry with myself when I was. Why can't I stand up for myself? Why am I still acting like I'm nine years old and keeping secrets?

One day, I built up enough courage to tell my manager. The following day, my co-worker confronted me and told me if I messed with him, I would be the one to lose my job, not him.

> *I built up enough courage to tell my manager.*

I believed him. I never liked confrontations, so I made no mention of it again. My manager must have confronted him. That day, I realized every time I spoke up, it never turned out the way I expected.

My days at work got a little better because he stopped verbally harassing me. Instead, he would give me an evil look. I preferred that. I tried my best to stay away when I could.

Eventually, I left that job and moved to another company. I couldn't work under those conditions anymore. I was glad to move on and find something better. Well, at least, that's what I hoped for. In this new company, males surrounded me. How did I not realize that when I was being interviewed? As a new employee, all the attention was on me. I endured having to hear those dreaded words, "You are pretty" or "You are beautiful." Of course, I pretended I appreciated the compliments, but I really didn't.

I developed a close relationship with one of my co-workers. This helped my days to be a little more relaxing.

She was humorous, and you can say she was my protector on the job. If she felt anyone was hanging around my desk too much, she would always check to see what was going on. She didn't know about my past, but she seemed to sense I needed protection.

Endless Cycle

A guy who worked at the company would often hang around my desk, but it was a norm for him to be in our office. However, I noticed something queer about him. He always had his hand in his pants. That made me feel very uncomfortable. One day, I worked late, and he came to my desk with his hand in his pants. I packed up and went home. I asked God again, "Why me? Why can't men just leave me alone?" It seemed like an endless cycle. Once again, I feared going to work and was under pressure to avoid this person.

> *Why can't men just leave me alone?*

During this time, my mom became extremely ill; her doctor diagnosed her with renal failure. I was depressed. Nothing seemed to make me happy anymore. I knew we would all have to take care of our parents if they lived long enough to become elderly, but my mother was far from being old; she was only 55 years old. I wasn't ready for the responsibility of taking care of a parent.

In many ways, I was still my nine-year-old self craving for someone to understand and take care of me. But I had to adjust my life and get used to the changes. I didn't enjoy watching my mom go through her illness. Even though she was the one who was ill, I felt I was being attacked again. "Wow, how many more situations do I need to deal with?"

I didn't know who I was. An abundance of negative thoughts were in control reminding me nothing good was supposed to happen to me. I went to work under pressure thinking about my mom and fearful of my male co-worker. Those days, I had migraines almost every day. I lost my appetite. It seemed everyone was seeing the sun outside, while darkness surrounded me. All I wanted was a normal life.

One day, I told my close co-worker what the male coworker was doing. She asked me a question that embarrassed me because I always asked myself that very question but never had an answer. She asked, "Why didn't you just tell him to move, ask him what he was doing or tell him to stop?" I told her I didn't know why. Just saying those words hurt me to my soul. I worried that she might look at me differently. She considered me to be a bright person with common sense but now, she was probably saying this dumb young woman can't even defend herself. It was true; I didn't defend myself.

> "Why didn't you just tell him to stop?"

An Unthinkable Act

From that day on when she saw him around my desk, she would turn him away. I was relieved to know I had someone there to protect me. However, one day she was absent and the pervert came to my desk. I saw him in the corner of my eyes as he put his hands in his pants. I was shouting at myself inside to tell him to move but no words came out of my mouth. Eventually, he pulled out his private part and masturbated right in front of me. I was horrified! That nine-year-old little girl took over me, and I couldn't move or say anything. I numbed myself to soothe the pain I was feeling.

When he left, I stayed there frozen in utter disbelief and fear. I didn't know how much more I could take. I was weak mentally and physically. I gave up on wondering why me. Quickly, I gathered my thoughts and belongings and headed home. That day, it was hard for me to pretend that everything was fine, so I told my husband. He was furious and insisted I tell my manager, but I told him I couldn't do that. He gave me an ultimatum, either I tell my manager or he was going on my job for the guy. I didn't want him to come to my job to hurt my co-worker.

"People won't believe you; it's our little secret." Those words from my abusive teacher replayed in my mind over

I didn't know how much more I could take.

and over again. Even though these men never told me it was our secret, I still believed it was. The lie the teacher told me was rooted in my being. Satan clouded my mind with bad thoughts, "See, this is why your teacher told you it's our little secret. When it's a secret, you don't have to worry about confrontation or getting hurt." I knew my husband was serious, and I didn't sleep at all that night. I lay there in fear, not knowing what would happen when I arrived at work the following day. I knew if my husband came to my job, it would not be good for my co-worker.

I opted to tell my manager. I went into her office trembling but through all the tears, I got my words out. I felt so humiliated because I was in a vulnerable state and people saw exactly how I was feeling. Normally, I covered that well. I was very good at hiding my feelings but this day, I couldn't hold them back.

My co-worker heard me crying, and she came right into the office. She didn't wait for my manager to give her the permission to enter. After learning what happened, she had this look of disappointment. I felt even more humiliated, but later, I realized she wasn't disappointed with me but with my male co-worker.

I wanted the ground to swallow me up. I wanted to stop breathing. I wanted to faint because I was so embarrassed that I lost my composure at work.

Tell Your Truth

Eventually, I got myself together and my manager gave me the rest of the day off. I felt proud and relieved that I could tell my husband I spoke up and told my manager. It felt good to know I didn't keep it a secret. My husband hugged me and told me he was proud of me. It felt so good to hear that. In a split second, I felt as if he was my father hugging me and telling me he was proud of me. However, I snapped out of it quickly and had a revelation. After being with my husband for 17 years, ten of those years married, I finally realized I was looking to my husband to be a father figure, to be that father I was longing for. I had to come to grips with the truth: my husband couldn't fill the void my father created in my life.

I knew I needed help, but I dismissed the thought because I didn't want to put myself through counseling again. I didn't think counseling was beneficial for me at that time.

I went to work the following day not knowing what to expect. My manager called me into a meeting with the director. He offered his apologies and regrets about the incident. They immediately fired my colleague, which was a bittersweet moment. I was relieved for me yet sorry he didn't have a job anymore. They offered me counseling sessions, but I refused.

I tried to move on and work at my desk, but it was difficult. I kept on having flashbacks and felt dirty sitting there. My manager allowed me to move to another cubicle for a while. But after a few days, I moved back to my cubicle. I decided to block those memories and bury them with all the others.

What a Relief

Later on, I left that job and moved on to another. This new environment was different; everyone was professional and cordial with each other. It was a relief.

During my early years at this job, my mom became ill again. I started to understand the scripture verse where Paul said:

> His grace is sufficient for me, for in my weakness he is strong. (2 Corinthians 12:9)

My mom was in the hospital for four months. While there, she could not walk and her memory failed. Some days, it was very difficult to visit because she didn't remember me. Being the only child, I had a lot of support from my family while she was in the hospital. Even with all the support, I became overwhelmed with emptiness and sadness. But God's grace carried me through despite depression and darkness. His grace comforted me and allowed me to perform on my job. It strengthened me to visit my mother every day. God's grace kept me from losing my mind.

At this point, I started to reflect on my life. As far back as five years old, people would say to my mom, "Is Aniskha okay? She doesn't smile." Or they would say, "She looks so sad." Even though I was young, it frustrated me because I wanted people to leave me alone and stop asking my mom questions. But they were right. I was sad most of the time. I encountered moments of happiness, but my life was one of sadness.

> *God's grace kept me from losing my mind.*

I finally figured it out! Sadness and emptiness would always be me. That was my reality. So I accepted it and stopped fighting.

The Consequence

Once I accepted Satan's lie, I lived it. Panic attacks became frequent. I went to my doctor regularly with complaints of not being able to breathe. Some days, I had to use a nebulizer because by the time I got there, I was overexerted and needed help to relax and breathe properly. She questioned me about my daily routine and wanted to know if all was well at home. I told her my mom was in the hospital for about three months.

My doctor associated the panic attacks with the trauma of dealing with an ill parent and having to cope with work and home. I wanted to tell her so much more but the fear of being judged or looked down on kept me from doing so.

One day, I visited Mom. I usually went there straight after work every day and was strong but not this day. I stood there by her bedside, and she looked at me clueless. I could not handle seeing her that way, so I walked out and left. I walked to my car with tears in my eyes, and I cried all the way home. When I got home, I went straight into my mom's room. No one else was at home. I sat in her chair, looked at her picture, and cried. For the three months she was in the hospital, I didn't really show my emotions to anyone. This was the first time I really cried and cried out to God as if my mom had died.

> *Once I accepted Satan's lie, I lived it.*

The phone rang. It was one of my older cousins who is a nurse. She was very supportive in making sure my mom was treated well at the hospital. When I said hello, she heard my cries and asked me what I wanted her to do. I said nothing. I told her I wanted my mother back. She agreed she wanted the same thing, and she was on her way to be with me. I cried and begged the Lord to please bring my mom back. While I was crying out to God, one of my mom's friends whom I affectionately call "Auntie" telephoned me and asked how I was doing.

This was the first time since my mom was in the hospital that I admitted I wasn't doing well. I would normally give a warm smile and say I was good or hanging in there. She told me she was coming over. When she arrived, I couldn't speak or control myself. I rested in her arms and cried. Eventually, after an hour or so, I was all right, and I composed myself because my boys were on their way home. My cousin never showed up. I learned later that because I was crying, she broke down too.

He Heard My Cry

Early the next morning, I got a call from my other cousin who is also a nurse. She worked the night shift, so she would check on my mom before she left the following morning. I used to be very afraid when my phone rang because I knew it could be bad news. When I answered the phone, I heard a weak, frail voice calling my name. I realized it was my mother. That was the best gift ever. It was a miracle. Just to hear her talk and remember me was evidence God had answered my prayer. He heard my cry.

> In my distress I called to the Lord; I cried to my God for help. From his temple he heard my voice; my cry came before him, into his ears. (Psalm 18:6)

Two days later, my mom's friend who came to me that evening shared her story. She is also a nurse. She said the same day I was crying, she had visited mom the evening before she left work. She didn't think my mom would have made it through that night because of what she observed. She said when she heard my mom talking the following day, she knew it was only God who touched her. Later, when my mom really talked, she said she remembered that night when God touched her. Never doubt God. He is real! He showed Himself to my mom, me, and others around who were involved in her life during that time.

I had a talk with Sarah; this time, I could not pretend. She said those words again, "See a counselor." She also told me she was afraid I would crash or have a nervous breakdown. She was correct about the nervous breakdown. I felt as if it was about to happen, but I still refused to seek help. I would pray and ask God for help but was I listening to God to get my answer? At that point in time, He was probably saying, "Listen to your friend and seek counseling."

The resentment in my heart made it harder to hear from God.

Still, I didn't want to face the truth about what God was saying because I was carrying so much guilt and shame. The resentment in my heart made it even harder to hear from God. I professed to be a Christian, but did I trust God?

After speaking to Sarah, I usually felt a little better even though she irritated me by attempting to get me to get therapy. However, I didn't feel better this time; I felt worse. I started to feel sorry for myself and said it won't get any easier.

Chapter 9

THERE'S ONLY ONE WAY OUT

Time went on. I did my daily routines, but I felt dead. I was becoming numb to everyone and everything around me. I hit rock bottom but even though Satan tried to trap me, someone was praying for me. God was fighting my battles.

I had dark thoughts swirling around in my mind. One day, I pictured my family living without me. I thought they would be better off if I wasn't there. I fought those thoughts in my head and told myself my kids needed me, and it would wreck my mom if I was not in her life.

I tried to convince myself that my husband would not need me either. Despite all that was going on, Perry loved me very much. I knew this but sometimes I wished he didn't. That way, I could comfort myself into believing I didn't have to make it work because he didn't love me. Despite my neglect, he always tried to make me happy and would constantly say these three words, "I love you."

That made me feel worse sometimes. How could he love me yet not understand why I felt the way I did?

As I alluded to earlier, my new job environment was amazing. There were no verbal or physical attacks. Everyone was just professional. The previous attacks still upset me though, but I tried my best to relax. I made sure I wasn't visible to my colleagues. I stayed at my desk, barely interacted with anyone and then headed home.

> *He would constantly say, "I love you."*

Exhausting Pretense

One day at work, I started to feel overwhelmed and depressed. I felt hopeless. I would take breaks to go to the bathroom to cry and compose myself before I went back to my desk. Though I would have a smile on my face and share a humorous conversation with my manager, inside, I was losing hope. I was exhausted every day after work because I had to pretend all day that I was fine.

I would go home and be silent. I didn't talk much with Perry or my mom. I also had little interaction with my boys whom I loved. I didn't have it in me to play with them, sit and help with homework or make sure they ate. I wanted freedom and hoped that I could become invisible to my family. I didn't want them to need me anymore.

While dropping the boys off at baseball practice one day, I stopped at a convenience store to purchase drinks. As I approached one aisle, I got the shock of my life. I saw my primary school teacher. We looked each other in the eye and continued walking. I remained calm, got the drinks, and left the store.

I told my husband what happened that day. After almost 28 years, I saw this man, and we both remembered each other. The surprised expression on his face was an indication he remembered me. I knew it was him because I could never forget his face. My husband asked how I felt, but I wasn't sure about my emotions. When I saw him, I had the same reaction as when I was around him in school—numb. I didn't realize that seeing him again would change my life forever. The numbness wore off a few days later.

The Floodgate

All the memories I locked away were trying to escape from the vault. This was a big, heavy-duty vault with layers of codes and locks. I promised myself I would not open it—the memories were too painful. Now, I felt as if I was losing control. The memories wanted to be released, but I fought tooth and nail to keep the vault locked. This fight became

> *All the memories I locked away were trying to escape.*

so strenuous I had nightmares. The anxiety attacks were more frequent and intense.

One Saturday afternoon, I was sitting at home and the voice in my head became clearer and more aggressive. It reminded me it wouldn't get better. It said, "Why do you want to hang around; you should leave." I would normally disagree with this voice and shake it off but that day, it was convincing.

Listen, when God has a plan for your life, the Devil will try to destroy it but that's all he can do. God has already won the victory. Although I agreed with this voice, the other voice was telling me to fight. But this soft voice was overshadowed by the voice of destruction.

Trusting Relationship

My doctor and I grew closer because I took my boys to her office regularly to ensure they were in good health. This sparked a trusting relationship between us. She gave me her cell number in case anything happened to the boys I could reach her. That day, I texted her. I told her I was having suicidal thoughts, and I was not sure what to do. After sending the text, I had regrets. I wanted to take it back, but I couldn't. I figured it was just one of those moments when I doubted myself and the feeling didn't really exist. Sometimes, I would doubt what happened to me in primary school. I started to convince myself that I made it all up.

The week went on. I didn't get a reply, and I was still having those feelings. I visited my doctor because of the anxiety attacks. She didn't mention receiving my text message, and I didn't ask if she did. I wasn't sure how to have that conversation, so I stayed quiet. She would always ask what triggered the attacks. Of course, I would blame it on work, even though the only place I felt comfortable was at work. Even as an adult, I was too timid to tell the truth.

Guess What?

Every day at home, I would distance myself more and more believing the lie of Satan that I was not needed. One day, while I was sitting in the front room feeling hopeless and wishing to die, my oldest son, who was nine at the time, walked up and said, "Mommy, guess what? God loves you, and I love you too." I hugged and assured him I loved him very much. I was so caught up in my feelings, I didn't realize the impact of those words and how God was using my child to show His love for me.

Time went on and the voice grew stronger and more demanding. It kept reminding me this is it! It will never get better, and I couldn't continue to live. I came home one day and went straight to bed. I could not pretend that day. I wanted some alone time.

My youngest son was about six; he would always follow me. We used to call him my shadow. He came into the room. Talking a lot was not something he did (that was my oldest son's area of expertise), but we had a long conversation.

Take Me

While he sat there talking and playing with his toys, I looked at him and begged the Lord to take me, to just let me go to sleep and never wake up again. I told Him my boys would be fine; they have a family who loves them very much. I lay there weak and frustrated.

I thank God for not granting my desire. My heart's desire didn't line up with God's will for my life and there was no glory in it for Him. I thank the Lord it was not in His will to let me die. I continued to live with the demanding voice in my head. Though I smiled each day, I was more depressed than ever and my heart was bleeding.

> Let me go to sleep and never wake up again.

The road leading to my workplace had a dock and beach on one side. One day, while heading to work, the voice told me to drive my jeep off the road into the water. It said people will understand just what I had to deal with.

I cried because it was a struggle not to listen to that voice. But God kept and delivered me again.

In the Knick of Time

I got a call from a number I didn't recognize; it was my doctor. She said she had given her cell phone with the number I had to her daughter who was off to college. Her daughter came home and told her about the text. This was a month later. She asked me if I was still having those thoughts, and I told her yes. Talk about God's perfect timing for me to receive that call that day. She told me she would make an appointment with a doctor she wanted me to see. I agreed.

I reached out to Sarah, and I told her what was happening. I almost felt she wanted to say I told you so, but she didn't. She begged me to attend counseling and be very honest about every aspect of my life. The conversation became heated *I was in denial and afraid to face my pain.* because I still didn't understand why she felt counseling would work. She believes in being transparent and speaking the truth because the truth will set you free. She explained that Satan told me so many lies from a child that I needed to counter them with the truth.

For the next few days, she made it her duty to talk with me every day. Most days, I was angry with her because

I felt she was attacking me. She was the one person I expected to understand me. Nevertheless, even though I was angry, I knew she loved me and wanted the best life God has for me. I was angry because I was in denial and afraid to face my pain and fears.

The appointment for me to see the doctor was never made, but I didn't push the issue. The sleepless nights continued, and I was exhausted. I was too afraid to sleep because the nightmares were horrible. The anxiety attacks were frequent, and I was paranoid all the time. I was a total mess inside. I needed freedom and the only way out was for me to take my life.

Chapter 10
....

GOD WAS ALWAYS THERE

One morning in July 2014, on my way to work, the demanding voice said again, "It's time. Let's just end this. Why do you want to go on living like this?" It also said, "Something terrible is bound to happen to you very soon again."

I went to the beach across from my work again thinking about driving my jeep off the ramp into the waters. Thankfully, even though that demanding voice was there, another voice was saying, "No, don't do it!"

With this fierce battle raging in my head, I was on the brink of a nervous breakdown. I made up my mind to drive over the ramp. But instead, I pulled to the side and stopped. I was a mess, weeping, and trembling.

I couldn't go to work. Instead, I built up the courage I needed to call my doctor. Normally, it was difficult to reach her by phone but if you sent her a text, she would respond once she could. God was in the midst of my struggle; the phone rang, and she answered on the second ring. I managed to tell her I couldn't do this anymore. I was tired, and I wanted it to stop. She asked me where I was, and I gave her my location. She told me not to move, and she would call me back.

What she didn't realize was I couldn't move. It was as if someone was there stopping me from driving. This was another act of God's love and faithfulness toward me. He was protecting me from what could have been worse. I could not move my vehicle. I was supposed to drive into the water, not park my car on the side.

She called back and told me she had reached my friend Amber, and she was on the way. I sat there and waited. When Amber arrived, she took me to my doctor. I hadn't spoken with Amber for a while, so she wasn't aware of what was going on.

The Revelation

At the doctor's office, I finally opened up and revealed the truth. I told the doctor what happened in primary school and that I had seen the teacher recently. I just kept saying, "I should not have gone with him. I disobeyed my mom. I was supposed to stay at the Sports Center." It was as if that ten-year-old just wanted to get punished for what she did and move on. The doctor finally understood why

I was having all the anxiety attacks and was frequently in her office for migraines or chest pain.

She asked me if I had attended the doctor she referred me to. I told her no one called me about it. She was surprised and upset because she said she had made the appointment.

While I was sitting there, she called and made another appointment. She told them it was urgent, and they scheduled a time for the following day.

She also gave me some medication to help me relax and get some sleep. I went by Amber's house instead of going home to rest and to compose myself for a while. Then I went home to my family. My husband picked me up, and I told him what happened but didn't provide all the details because I wasn't sure he understood what I was going through. I told him about the counseling, and he was happy I agreed to go.

My mind was now racing. I was afraid and upset because I had let my guard down. I was also disappointed with myself for being vulnerable in front of the doctor. I wasn't sure I really wanted to go to counseling at this point, but I felt a tugging. That same weak, frail voice was telling me I needed to go. However, the demanding voice was also trying to persuade me it made no sense and would not work. The voice kept saying it was a waste of time and would be just like all the other occasions I went for counseling.

I spoke with Sarah that evening. She was elated to know I was going. She encouraged me to tell the truth because that was the only way it would work. She reminded me God wanted me to be free from all the lies Satan had planted in my mind that caused the guilt and shame. I heard her but still did not agree with her fully. I didn't have the energy to argue, so I just listened. That night, I managed to get a few hours of sleep after being deprived for so many weeks.

I went to work the following day. My appointment was at the end of the day. I was extremely nervous when I got there. I wanted to cancel the appointment because I didn't feel able to do it anymore. When my name got called, my heart was racing. I felt I was going to have an anxiety attack while walking to the room.

This Would Be Different

The doctor introduced himself and then he asked the question professionals like to ask, "So what brings you here today?" I was totally turned off. Here I go again—the same questions they learned to ask all their patients while they were at university. But before I could answer, he said something that made me believe this session would be different from the others I attended. He said, "I need you to know your presence here is no coincidence. This is where God wants you to be at this time in your life. So I need you to trust God and trust me to help you."

When he said that the vault I had all the bad memories tucked away in opened. I had no will power to keep it closed. I started talking about my teacher and my dad. I blamed myself out loud. I wanted to stop but I couldn't; the words were just flowing out. I told him I hated myself. I hated my father. I always felt dirty and nothing took those feelings away. I started to panic and couldn't breathe. Immediately, he taught me how to control my breathing.

> *I need you to trust God and trust me to help you.*

Panic attacks make us feel we can't breathe or catch our breath; that's because we forget to exhale. I learned that day to take deep breaths by slowly inhaling through my nose and consciously exhaling through my mouth. I continued this pattern while relaxing my mind and it worked.

Once the panic attack stopped, he continued. He asked me a very interesting question—if I could remember the last time I was truly happy without feeling any sadness. I thought about my wedding and the birth of my kids. I was going to give him that answer.

Naked?

Then I heard Sarah's voice reminding me to be honest and open. While I was hearing her voice, he said to me, "I am going to need you to be naked before me." Naked? Why did he use that word? I froze. I thought he was flirting with me. So I put up a protective wall and reminded myself that nothing good will happen to me.

I think he saw the look of emptiness and disappointment on my face. He asked me if I understood what he meant by being naked with him. I managed to say, "no" very faintly. He explained he needed me to be open and honest with him and myself because he wasn't there to judge me. He said no one can tell me how to feel or what to think, but I do have the power to control my feelings and thoughts. He told me to relax and think about the question again. I thought about it, and it definitely wasn't my wedding or my sons' birth. Even though I was happy on those special days, I still felt sadness and emptiness inside. Trying to answer that question was too difficult. I doubted if I could answer. My head hurt.

It was obvious I was struggling, so he asked me easier questions. He asked me where I worked, what I did at work, how many children I have and their ages. Eventually, he asked me the same question again—when was the last time I felt true happiness without any sadness. I took a deep breath and decided to really think about it. I told him I don't ever remember truly being happy. I said I could remember as far back as going to kindergarten for the first time. I was excited to go but not sure I was really happy. I told him I can remember from the age of five people asking my mom why I looked sad and how frustrated I became when I heard that question.

Chapter 11

BAD THOUGHTS VS. GOOD THOUGHTS

During my first session, the doctor diagnosed me with dysthymic disorder, which is double depression. It's a depressed mood accompanied by one or two other symptoms of clinical depression. Dysthymic disorder is described as a "veil of sadness," which occurs every day and persists for many years. It also increases the risk of suicidal thoughts.

My doctor said I was experiencing depression from trauma and daily feelings of sadness for all those years. He told me I can be happy and remove the sadness, but it would take a lot of work. He asked me if I was ready to work toward being whole and live the life God wants me to live. He explained I could do this through cognitive-behavioral therapy. This is psychotherapy where negative thought patterns about self and the world are challenged to alter unwanted behavioral patterns or treat mood disorders such as depression. This counseling felt different. I was ready to take on the challenge, but I was still skeptical about whether or not it would work.

Doubts aside, I agreed to follow the doctor's advice. He reminded me to be naked and truthful with him. Even though he explained the word "naked" previously, hearing it still made me feel gross. I wished he would use another term like transparent, but I didn't build up the courage to tell him.

He assigned homework that day. I sat there and before he told me what the homework would be, I had concluded I wasn't doing it. I was too drained emotionally and tired to do any homework.

Just Feelings

It was almost as if this man was reading my mind that day. He told me the homework was important, and he knew I didn't feel as if I had the energy to complete it, but I had to push beyond my feelings. That day, I learned something very important. Our feelings are just feelings. We should not allow them to dictate our lives because we have complete control over them. My doctor gave an example.

We determine what we need to do despite how we feel.

He said, "You know you have to go to work because that pays the bills. If you wake up one morning and don't feel like going to work, do you listen to that feeling or do you go to work?"

I answered, "Well, I would go to work despite how I felt."

He responded, "Yes, you are right. So as with everything else in life, our feelings don't dictate what we do or should not do. We control our minds and determine what we need to do despite how we feel about it."

Complete Control

At first, when he said this, it didn't make complete sense. However, my feelings were controlling and determining what I did daily, so he was right. It was a relief to know there was a possibility that one day, I could have complete control over my feelings.

My homework for that week and going forward was to write in a journal every day what I felt and what negative thoughts were on my mind during that day. I also had to write a good thought to cancel out the negative thoughts and feelings. We all have feelings whether they are those of sadness, disappointment, happiness, excitement or fear. These emotions affect the way we think and whether we produce positive or negative thoughts. I

> *I had to learn how to set my mind on positive things.*

produced more negative thoughts. Hence, I had to learn how to set my mind on positive things.

> Finally, brothers and sisters, whatever is true, whatever is noble, whatever is right, whatever is pure, whatever is lovely, whatever is admirable if anything is excellent or praiseworthy think about such things.
> (Philippians 4:8)

I was not confident about this at first. However, this exercise was a start for me to learn how to take authority over my mind and control my thoughts and feelings. My doctor reminded me that God loves me, and I am fearfully and wonderfully made by Him.

At the end of my session, he prescribed medication for the depression and something to help with the anxiety attacks. I wasn't too keen on taking the medicine because I had heard negative things about it. It was also disturbing to know I had to rely on it. I didn't voice my concerns to the doctor. I simply accepted the prescription and that was the end of my first session. I left there, and even though I did not want to be on medication, I felt I was ready to continue with the sessions.

By the time I reached home, my excitement had faded. I thought about the medications I didn't want to take and his use of the word "naked." I didn't follow his advice about not allowing my feelings to control what I did or didn't do.

I reached out to my general doctor and asked her about the medications. I told her I didn't want to take them because of all the side effects. She told me in her soft, stern voice that I needed them, and I wouldn't be on the medicines long enough for them to negatively affect me. She asked me to trust the process and do what the doctor said. I agreed. I took the pills for a few weeks and then stopped.

Just that Word

I also told her I wanted counseling, but I didn't like his approach. I explained I was not comfortable with him using the word "naked" and asked if anyone else could help me. Truthfully, I didn't want to go to anyone else, but I had to make it sound good. I knew she would not agree with me giving up on counseling. She assured me he was the right one for me and that she would talk to him.

She reached out to him, and he apologized at my next session. He explained he needed me to be transparent with him and to remember what he said—he was not there to judge me. He also repeated that no one could tell me how I should feel and my feelings matter. All he wanted me to do was practice controlling my feelings. I was not to let them cause me to make bad choices or miss out on what the Lord has for me. His response surprised me. I thought he would have been upset because I reached out to my other doctor, not him. He wasn't. Evidently, he wasn't there to judge me. I believed him. In this session, he went through my homework, and we discussed a few journal entries.

I wrote in my journal almost every day. Below are a few excerpts:

Sept 11, 2014, 5:30 am

Negative thoughts: Yesterday was rough. Why did that man have to take my innocence away from me at such a young age? I didn't deserve that; no child does. Now, I am living with nasty thoughts and feelings in my head. I don't like that.

Good thought: I have none; that's just facts.

Sept 11, 2014, 6:42 pm

Negative thoughts: Need someone to talk to but everyone is busy or they don't understand me. I don't understand me. I am just a wimp and a cry baby looking for attention.

Good thought: One day, I won't need anyone's attention.

Sept 14, 2014, 7:17 am

Negative thoughts: I don't want to get out of bed. I don't feel like doing anything. I just want to lay here and pretend nothing exists.

Good thought: None.

Sept 15, 2014, 9:36 pm

Negative thoughts: Why did I let that man violate my privacy at work? I can't even stand up for myself. Am I a magnet to harassment from men? Primary school, high school, work—why?

Good thought: Not all men are the same. My husband is a good man.

Sept 23, 2014, 6:07 am

Negative thoughts: I feel like I am going crazy inside. I must keep up this persona as if I am happy and want to work. I don't feel like talking; I don't even want to work. I'm just tired of pretending.

Good thought: None.

Undated

Negative thought: I heard on the news today that a 14-year-old girl committed suicide. That hurt me so much inside because I truly know the feeling. I know the only reasons

I have not overdosed are because of holding on to God, my husband, and my boys. I am really tired. I just want to get away for a while so I can be free to cry all day and not get out of bed if I didn't want to. It is hard feeling sad and hopeless and having to pretend to the world that I am okay.

Good thought: Writing is supposed to make you feel better but not tonight.

Chapter 12
....

OPENING THE VAULT

My counseling sessions were held once a week. The first three months were painful because I had to give details about everything that had happened. One night after my session, I reached out to my general doctor and told her I didn't want to go to counseling anymore. She encouraged me to trust the process. In a gentle, professional way, she said it was not an option. I had to do it.

In the beginning, I made up excuses about why I shouldn't go. However, my strong support team of five—two of them being my husband and Sarah—were not convinced by my excuses.

At these sessions, we dealt with a lot of issues, but the focus was on my self-worth, forgiving my dad, and learning how to live after molestation and sexual harassment.

Self-worth

I was reminded that I was fearfully and wonderfully made, and God had a plan and purpose for my life. God has a plan for everyone's life. He did not put any of us on this earth to suffer. Satan also has a plan to kill and destroy us.

> *I started to produce more positive thoughts.*

Every time I looked in the mirror I felt disgusted by what I saw: failure, scars, low self-esteem, regrets, guilt, and shame. I saw an ugly person. Now, I had to learn to realign my perceptions about myself with what God thought of me. I started to produce more positive thoughts like these:

- If I draw near to God, He will draw nearer to me
- I can do all things through Christ who strengthens me
- I am an overcomer

I had to learn that God is not there waiting to whip me with a stick, look down on me or accuse me. He isn't there to condemn me.

> For God did not send his Son into the world to condemn the world, but to save the world through him. (John 3:17)

God is love. He is waiting with open arms for me to surrender all the hurt, shame, and guilt to Him. He doesn't want me to carry all these burdens on my own. Instead, He wants me to give them all to Him. That sounded so easy but how could I give it all to Him and allow myself to be just me without pretending.

I was encouraged by the book *Victory over Darkness* by Neil T. Anderson. It helped me to understand who I am in Christ. It also provided quotes with scripture references that reminded me of who I am in Christ. Each day, I made the following declarations:

- I have been adopted as God's child (Ephesians 1:5)
- I have been redeemed and forgiven of all my sins (Galatians 1:4)
- I am free from condemnation (Romans 8:1-2)
- I am born of God and the Evil One cannot touch me (1 John 5:18)—I love this declaration
- I have been chosen and appointed to bear fruit (John 15:16)

These verses helped calm my fears and settle the suicidal thoughts. I didn't feel as hopeless, and I was thinking, "Am I on this earth for a good cause?"

With all my flaws, I had to learn to love me. God loves me. He knew just who I would be, and He loves me with all my flaws. If I don't love myself, I can't accept love from others.

Forgiving My Dad

My doctor said at one of the sessions that after forgiving my father, I had two options: having a relationship with my dad or just forgiving him and moving on. That was a tough decision because I wanted a relationship with my father for so long, but I had grown out of it. Now, I had to deal with those thoughts and emotions again.

I decided to forgive my father and work on developing a relationship with him. Despite how I felt, he was my father, and I loved him very much. I thought about this scripture again:

> Honor your father and your mother, so that you may live long in the land the Lord your God is giving you. (Exodus 20:12)

I accepted I couldn't rebuild a relationship from the past but moving forward, I could have an adult relationship with my dad. This was scary for me because I didn't want to get hurt if it didn't work out. Anyway, I held on to this scripture:

> And we know that all things work together for the good to those who love God, to those who have been called according to His purpose. (Romans 8:28)

When I prayed and forgave my father, I felt a burden lifted. I wasn't sure if I should get excited because I wanted to be protective of my feelings. I was still taking baby steps to override negative thoughts with good thoughts and what God said about me. I can tell you now that as of today, my dad and I have a much healthier relationship.

> When I forgave my father, a burden lifted.

My dad has a great sense of humor that I enjoy, and he has built a strong relationship with Perry. If I didn't allow the Lord to work in me and show me it's not too late to have a relationship, I would have still been living with a void no one else could fill. Don't get me wrong; God can fill all our emptiness but having this relationship with my dad was the desire of my heart. God gave it to me through forgiveness.

When my father first told me he loved me, my heart was so full I wanted to cry. I finally heard the words I longed to hear from my childhood. I knew he loved me. Wow, good things can really happen to me!

Molestation and Sexual Harassment

This was the longest part of my counseling sessions. Many days, I cried because I didn't want to rehash those painful memories. Even though I had a support team that made sure I was going to counseling, an inner voice also inspired me to go. The demanding voice that once persuaded me to believe there was no reason for me to live was now fading away. It was being overruled by the weak voice to bring me hope. This voice was still soft, but it spoke with authority and love.

I had to unlock all those memories I stored far away. I asked my counselor, "Why am I always a target? Why can't I ever defend myself?" He explained it was because of the fear and trauma I went through as a child. He said once I am in a situation where I feel I am being violated, I shut down and allow fear to take over. In addition, fear doesn't allow me to speak up for myself or control what happens. This made sense, but I still wasn't sure how to change that.

More homework was assigned. I had to purposely remember everything that happened in the past and write it down, so I could share it at my sessions. I had to relive my experiences as a child; this was painful. One day, I was driving and had a vivid recollection of one of the incidents that happened in school. I relived all the pain, even though it wasn't happening at the time.

I pulled over on the side of the road in tears and called my counselor. I told him I was in pain, not just emotionally but also physically. I said I didn't understand what was going on, and I wanted it to stop. He assured me I was going to be all right and that was a necessary part of the healing process. He wanted me to relive every moment, so I could release everything I had been holding on to for so long. He reminded me it was all in the past and eventually, it will just be that. He said I will always have memories, but they won't affect me as they did at that time. He assured me again I would be all right and to remember it's just a feeling.

Before these sessions, I was having a lot of nightmares. After reliving this part of my life, the nightmares intensified. I concluded this was happening because I had to face the reality of what occurred and deal with the issues. I spoke to my counselor about it and he taught me how to control those nightmares.

Every time I had a nightmare, I had to rewrite my story. If I dreamed I was about to be attacked, I had to end the dream how I wanted it to end. I confess this was the most ridiculous thing I had ever heard. How could I rewrite a dream that is going on in my sleep? How could I subconsciously do this? I realized that most of the time, we know we are dreaming. We also subconsciously know we are sleeping, and it is all a dream. Some dreams are good because God gives His chosen vessels dreams and visions all the time. On the other hand, Satan tries to contaminate our minds with nightmares. You can feel yourself fighting to wake up, but it's a struggle.

> *I had to rewrite my story.*

Even though I thought this was ridiculous, I was ready to try it because I wanted to sleep on my own without taking pills. The first time, I had no success. I was frustrated and doubted if it would ever work. That's when the demanding voice of Satan said, "I told you so." But the positive voice reminded me to keep pressing. And I did. Eventually, it worked; it really worked!

Fighting Back

I remember in one of those nightmares I was being chased. The attacker caught me, pushed me to the ground and was about to get on top of me. I kicked him where it hurt and punched him in the face. I was so excited I couldn't wait to tell my counselor. With this method and prayer, the nightmares became less frequent. I slept better at night, and I could think and process everything much clearer.

After we got through all the memories of primary and high school, I had a new assignment. I had to learn to look in the mirror and see beyond the scars and filth. I had to say out loud every day, "I am fearfully and wonderfully made." Some days, I didn't want to do this exercise as I felt it wouldn't work. I would get angry because he gave me another ridiculous assignment.

> *The positive voice encouraged me to keep pressing on.*

I constantly saw scars. I always saw this unattractive girl with thick lips and filthy stains on her body. The negative voice tried again to convince me it would not work. The positive voice encouraged me to keep pressing on because God loves me with all my flaws. It kept saying God wants to cover all my scars and remove the filthy stains. The positive voice also told me God wants me to appreciate my lips because He uniquely designed them.

> For you created my inmost being, you knit
> me together in my mother's womb.
> (Psalm 139:13)

I had to stop blaming myself for wanting to be with my teacher and going with him to pick up the lunch that day. My counselor kept reminding me I was a child at the time. I knew I was a child, but I was disappointed with myself for choosing to go with my teacher because I should have known better.

They Are the Bad Guys

Dealing with each situation, counseling helped me realized the men were the culprits. They committed premeditated sins in their minds before I entered the picture. They had already made the choice to commit this sin whether it was against me or someone else, whether I had said no or put up a fight.

I had to accept and understand that the teacher was the perpetrator. No matter how intelligent I thought I was at the age of ten to exercise better judgment, I was not at fault. He had it all planned to prey on my innocence.

I learned that even though God is there and we might ask, "Why didn't God protect me because He knew I was innocent?" God allows all of us to make choices. Those men and my classmates made bad choices. I still struggle to figure out why they chose me. Despite Satan's attacks on my life to destroy me, my comfort is that God had a bigger plan.

Satan knows God has a plan for everyone on the earth. Hence, he strategizes to disrupt God's plan by any means possible. However, Satan's attempts to destroy me only made me a better person. God was there with me all the time. He was the weak voice I always heard. I described His voice as weak but the fact of the matter is it was not. I struggled to listen to the softer voice and allowed the other one to control me.

> *God was with me all the time.*

A New Me

I attended nine months of counseling that birthed a new me. I started off with weekly sessions and then to biweekly.

I was afraid to end counseling. Even though I didn't want to be there at first, I started to look forward to the sessions. Eventually, I felt free. When I wanted to cry, I cried. If I didn't want to talk that day, the counselor would do most of the talking, but he had his way of getting me to express what I was feeling.

At every session, he reminded me that God was my source; He truly loved me, and wouldn't condemn me. I was reminded again of this scripture:

> For God did not send his Son into the world to condemn the world, but to save the world through him. (John 3:17)

Throughout those sessions, I read more of God's Word and prayed for healing. I finally accepted that depression is really a sickness. During one of my last sessions, I asked, "Will I ever get healed from this?" He explained to me that depression is just like any other illness. He used hypertension as an example. You can experience a healthy life with hypertension, but you must make an effort to have a lifestyle that will keep your blood pressure balanced. He said it's the same with depression; I must work at it every day.

I had to remember not to let my feelings control my decisions. For example, if I get up feeling sad in the morning,

I should not let that sad feeling dictate what happens to me for the rest of the day. I should analyze why I feel sad and determine if it is the truth or another lie from Satan. I also have to determine in my mind that despite how I feel at a particular time, I will have a good day.

The counselor said meditation is important. If I feel overwhelmed, it is essential for me to relax and breathe. In addition, he advised that my support team is necessary for my success, and I should be transparent with them. I should not feel ashamed to reach out for help. I have learned that one of Satan's traps is to keep you in isolation and from the truth. Therefore, having a support team or person who can remind you of God's truth for your life is important.

I encourage you or anyone faced with trials to pray. Ask God to direct you to someone or people who can empower you and speak positively into your life when you are faced with challenges. My counselor also advised me to hold on to God's Word and recite scriptural text every day.

Doom and Gloom

Feeling as I did on the first day of kindergarten, I was now ready to face the world. A few months went by and I was doing well. But out of the blue, fear consumed me again. I thought, "I knew this was too good to be true." Doom and gloom overshadowed me, and I had this nagging feeling something would happen to snatch away my happiness. By this time, I felt lonely. My support team was no longer there for me or they needed a break. I had small panic attacks as I believed I would not make it. I wanted to go back to my counselor. Funny isn't it; the first time I visited, I didn't want to stay. Now, I felt I couldn't survive without going to my counselor.

> *It was time for me to move out of my comfort zone.*

I returned to counseling and felt protected again, but I knew it was time for me to move out of my comfort zone. I felt safe when I sat in that chair. I could be myself and not worry about being judged. But I knew it was time to leave that nine-year-old Nish behind. She will always be there but as a memory that reminds me of the goodness of God and where He has brought me from.

One day, a church friend invited me to a small gathering at her house. The older sister of her friend was in town. She was a well-known motivational speaker, coach, and trainer. Initially, I didn't want to attend because I wasn't yet comfortable interacting with others, but I built up enough courage to go.

An Ally

When the speaker introduced herself, she gave a little history of herself. She had migrated to the Bahamas at a young age to live with her mom. She talked about a teacher who made a positive impact on her life whom she wanted to reconnect with if she could. She called the teacher's name and instantly, I knew she was a teacher from my primary school. I asked her if she was referring to the teacher I knew and surely, she was. It amazed me to know we went to the same primary school.

At the end of her session, she shared her testimony about where God brought her from. When she told her story of how she was molested at primary school, I got chills. I am not sure I heard anything else she said because I knew God had answered my prayers. I met someone who had a similar experience at my primary school.

After the sessions, I inquired if I could ask her a few questions. I was very nervous, but she agreed. I told her I went to that same primary school and wanted to know if the person who molested her was my physical education teacher. She said yes. I felt happy and sad at the same time. I was sad to know she had such a horrible ordeal but happy to know what happened to me was real, not a fantasy. As I mentioned before, many times, I struggled with my thoughts. I would try to convince myself I was exaggerating and the molestation didn't occur. This really drove home the point that the men who hurt me made bad

> *What happened to me was real, not a fantasy.*

choices. My teacher was the undisciplined one. He was the perpetrator.

The speaker was at least four years ahead of me in school. While sharing our stories, we both realized the teacher preyed on young girls he felt needed attention. We were both saddened to know there probably were a lot more young girls who went through this same horrible experience. I was happy I wasn't alone; someone understood exactly how I felt.

Chapter 13

FREEDOM THROUGH CHRIST

A year had passed, and I still struggled with bouts of depression that put me in a dark place sometimes. Some days, I would speak words of hope and move away from that dark place. Other days, Satan had a stronghold on me. I would be in this dark place for a few days and literally feel as if a war was going on in my mind. I had headaches and felt trapped in a daze. This mental battle exhausted me, and I continued to suffer from a lack of sleep.

God is good! I say that because even though I had those encounters, I never had suicidal thoughts again. This constant battle went on for another year. I knew counseling would no longer help me because I had gathered all I needed from previous sessions. I had to trust God for my complete healing.

I started praying more and asking God for healing. My Bible study and devotional time were more active. I love the "YouVersion" app. I still use it today for my devotions. I looked for devotions tailored toward depression or the battle of the mind. Also, I read a lot of books that focused on depression, molestation or overcoming struggles. I loved to read Joyce Meyers' books because I always felt a connection to them. Even though I did all of this, I still struggled with depression.

What You Wish For

July 2016, I was exhausted mentally and physically. I returned from a baseball trip with my sons and immediately went back to work. I sat at my desk the first week after returning and said to God, "I am tired." I told Him I didn't see any way for me to get rest soon. I told Him I felt the only way I could get rest was to be admitted to the hospital. I didn't really desire this; it was just a way to express how I felt.

The Friday of that same week as I was about to get ready for work, I had an emergency. I had to go to my doctor and by that evening, I was being prepped to go into surgery the next morning. I told the surgeon I had a training event I was scheduled to attend for my company in Dallas in two weeks. I wanted to know if he felt I could go. There I was being prepped for surgery but focused on work and what I needed to accomplish. He explained the recovery time for that surgery was usually four to six weeks, but we would see how I recovered after the surgery and discuss further.

The surgery was successful. I didn't have to stay in the hospital afterward. I was sent home on bed rest. After my first checkup, the doctor gave me clearance to travel with special instructions. I could not under any circumstances lift anything heavy. I was happy about the news and agreed to follow his instructions. By the second day of my trip, I developed an infection. One of the stitches popped. When I returned, the doctor prescribed more medication, and I was put back on bed rest. That meant the healing process was extended, and I had to be on bed rest for three-and-a-half months.

The doctor told me something I will never forget. He said your mind, body, and soul need rest to have complete healing. That stood out, and I remember my talk with God about being tired. It is true; words have power and carry life or death. You must be careful what you ask for. The tongue is a powerful weapon.

> The tongue has the power of life and death,
> and those who love it will eat its fruit.
> (Proverbs 18:21)

During this period, I had a life-changing experience. On bed rest, I wasn't able to do anything but lie down and be still. God spoke to me, and I realized my life has a purpose. I needed to be still and quiet my mind, so I could hear from God. Sometimes, we are so busy and caught up with the trials of life, we often forget to be still and listen to God's voice.

He Was There

Psalm 91 gives me hope. I find comfort in knowing if I dwell in the shelter of the Most High, I do not need to be afraid because He is my refuge. In Him, I put all my trust. God is my refuge. He is my strength. He protects me from the Wicked One. He will send His angels to surround and cover me. God showed and reminded me that every time I was being molested or harassed, He was right there. He felt my pain, and cried when I cried. He held and comforted me. When I didn't feel I would make it home, He gave me the strength to do so. When I felt no one understood me, God did. He knew me before anyone else. He reminded me He would never put more on me than I could bear.

> No temptation has overtaken you except what is common to mankind. And God is faithful; he will not let you be tempted beyond what you can bear. But when you are tempted he will also provide a way out so that you can endure it. (1 Corinthians 10:13)

But he said to me, my grace is sufficient for you, for my power is made perfect in weakness. Therefore, I will boast all the more gladly about my weaknesses, so that Christ power can rest in me. (2 Corinthians 12:9)

I sat there in awe because I always prayed for God to take the depression away, but He reminded me that His grace is sufficient.

Grace and Mercy

When I am depressed now, He shows up with His grace and mercy. Grace is the strength that can only come from God. It allows me to endure the trials I face and resist the temptation to give up.

Grace is unmerited favor that comes from God. We are all sinners. We deserve to suffer and endure pain, but God's grace is a gift to us. His grace gives me the power to conquer depression whenever it attempts to weigh me down. He receives all the glory and honor.

> God reminded me of His love.

He gives me the strength to speak life into myself and my situation. I focus on Him through my praise and worship, instead of dwelling on the challenges I might be facing.

Consistently, as I lay in bed, God reminded me of His love. During this time, I totally released all the shame and guilt of my past. I handed it all to God. When doubts started to creep in, I remembered:

> For we fixed our eyes not in what is seen but on what is unseen, since what is seen is temporary, but what is unseen is eternal.
> (2 Corinthians 4:18)

While in bed, I remembered my counselor telling me about fear. Fear will stagnate your progress if you allow it. It is the one emotion that causes many people to live in mediocrity. Fear is the enemy of faith.

The Authority

I needed to build my self-confidence, have faith, and believe God is with me. He has given me the authority to speak up and face challenges. Whenever I am faced with fear now, I envision God saying this memory verse to me.

> The LORD himself goes before you and will be with you; he will never leave you nor forsake you. Do not be afraid; do not be discouraged. (Deuteronomy 3:18)

It is comforting to know that no matter what I must face, God will always be there. I remind myself that God is right there holding my hands and guiding me. I used to think I had to remove all fear before I could face a situation. However, I learned I had to face the situation with the fear but depend on God to carry me through. I remind myself that fear is of Satan, and I am a child of God. God has made me an overcomer.

I no longer have to be afraid to leave environments or situations that are not positive for me or pleasing to God. Also, I can feel confident about my decisions and not worry or be afraid of what others think. God has also given me a discerning spirit when it comes to men.

My doctor and I have developed a closer bond since the day I spoke with her about suicidal thoughts. She was a strong pillar in my support team. I am so glad I listened to her advice about trusting the process and being patient. It's best to listen and take wise counsel.

I trusted the process even though I could not see any light at the end of the tunnel. This is where faith came in for me. I could not see the end result, but I had to believe in the process and visualize myself being healed. Within the last year, while speaking with my doctor, she told me she felt most of my symptoms were psychosomatic. This is when most of your physical illnesses are caused by internal conflicts or stress. She explained she didn't mention it earlier because I wasn't ready to face the truth. I'm happy to report that I don't have those symptoms anymore. I stopped having all the chronic ailments that had me in my doctor's office frequently. I am free!

True Love

I also had a lot of time to reflect on my relationship with my husband. Despite the rough times in our marriage, I knew Perry loved me. I never once doubted his love for me. Sometimes I questioned if I could be the type of wife he deserves. I have grown to understand that love is a choice. Christ loved us despite our sins. Christ's love isn't based on His emotions; it is a choice. He died on the cross for us even though we deserved to be on the cross.

It is the same in our relationship; despite my flaws, Perry loves me. If his love for me was based on how he felt during difficult situations, our relationship would not have lasted. We have been married 16 years, and we're still going strong. God became the foundation of our marriage and Perry's devoted love for me. I have no problem being a submissive wife because of his love. I know he would go above and beyond for me. Our relationship is stronger today because of our trials. Trials come to test our strength and increase our knowledge about life. Because of what we had to overcome; it strengthened our bond.

The trials that came my way caused me to develop a close relationship with God. I experienced His great love toward me by daily spending time in His Word and talking with Him through prayer. Even though I had a great support team, God was my supreme supporter. He knew me better than anyone. He knew my next move or what was about to happen next. He is that inner voice I have learned to trust. I thank the Lord for everything because through it all, I experienced growth and development.

> Consider it pure joy, my brothers and sisters whenever you face trials of many kinds, because you know that the testing of your faith produces perseverance. Let perseverance finish its work so that you may be mature and complete, not lacking anything.
> (James 1:2-4)

When I went through my trials, I didn't comprehend the above verse. Now, I can appreciate it because I understand. I had to go through trials to be the person God wanted me to be. My trials were a process that pruned and made me more understanding and sympathetic toward others. It was preparation for a testimony God

> *My trials made me more understanding and sympathetic*

desires me to share with others. I can use my testimony to inspire and encourage those who face similar trials. I can influence them positively and let them know there is hope. They are overcomers through Christ Who gives us strength.

Good Use

Your trials will release unexpected abilities and growth. I never knew I had so much strength. I am stronger because I allowed God to be my strength and refuge. He is a present help in my time of trouble. It is joyful to see how God got all the glory and how He worked in my life even when I couldn't feel His presence, and I thought He had forsaken me. I can now use the pain that trapped me for many years for a purpose that is greater than me.

God turned me into a beautiful butterfly. I am no longer under Satan's control. When I look in the mirror, I see beauty and the wonderful work of my heavenly Father. I don't see filth or stains, but God's grace all over me. I don't see ugly because I know God looks at my heart, and I am living for God every day. I don't see thick lips but a smile that reminds me I should have no fear because my life is in God's hands. He will always be my protector.

ACKNOWLEDGMENTS

To my husband Perry who from day one always believed in me. When I spoke with him about leaving my day job to focus on my book, he was one hundred percent behind me. He told me to follow my dream and never give up.

Thank you for your continuous support, love, and commitment to helping this book become a success. Thanks for taking the time to read my manuscript and reminiscing with me on how far we have come. This was therapeutic to my soul; thank you so much.

To my oldest son Paris who reminded me one day that although I've always told him and his brother to follow their dreams, he doesn't see me following mine. Paris, thank you for those words that gave me the push every day to make sure I got this book completed. Thanks to you and Ayden for consistently asking me if I was working on my book. Thank you for following up and making sure it got completed.

Thanks to my writing coach and editor Sherique Dill. You have been a great coach from day one. I am so grateful God directed me to you, and you took on the task without hesitation. Thank you for believing in me despite all the challenges I had. You never doubted me even when I doubted myself. Your words of advice and wisdom have been great tools for me to complete this book.

> *Thank you for your support.*

Special thanks to my pastor, Mario Moxey, for his consistent obedience to the voice of God. Thank you for those powerful messages in church. Your sermon "Pursuing Your Dreams" in July 2018, got me started on this journey. You encouraged us to start pursuing our dreams by September 16, 2018. That is when I made a vow to God and took on the challenge of starting this book. I am so grateful for your teachings.

To my support team: Perry (my husband), Dr. Cindy Dorsett, Anna Roberts-Pilgrim, Kelly Roberts, Annette Rahming, and LoAnn Johnson—how can I express my gratitude to such a wonderful team? You spoke life into me when I could not speak life into myself. You never said, "You need to let it go" or "You need to move on." Rather, you always empathized with me. Your love and encouragement helped me through those nine months of counseling. I am thankful for the love you extended. God loves me as He gave me the best support team anyone can ask for.

To Anna, I'm grateful for our friendship. Dr. Barrett was my counselor throughout the day, but you were my consistent confidant. Thank you for never giving up on me. Although some days you were tired, you made sure I was doing well first before you ended your day.

To my counselor, Dr. Timothy Barrett, I am grateful for the knowledge you instilled in me. I am also thankful you counseled me based on the Word of God. I will never forget the great enthusiasm you had when you spoke about God and how much He loves us. If I didn't believe God loved me, your excitement for God had a domino effect; it captured my heart.

To my sister in Christ, Krista Deveaux, thanks for your faith in Christ, as well as your prayers and excitement whenever I talked about this book. You have taught me in so many ways how to have radical faith, which allowed me to see this book completed.

To Elder Tiffany Edgecombe, thank you for your willingness to assist and referring me to Christian Living Books.

To all my family and friends who have impacted my life with encouraging words, and positive thoughts—thank you.

I pray God's blessings on each of you for helping me through my journey and making this book a great success.

Special thanks to you, the reader, for your support. This book couldn't have been successful without you.

To God, my heavenly Father, who is the great Author and inspiration for me to write and finish this book. Thank You for using me as one of Your vessels to show others Your love and compassion for us. Thank You for never giving up on me. You have always had a plan and purpose for my life.

ABOUT THE AUTHOR

Aniskha Johnson was born and raised in Nassau, Bahamas. She and her husband Perry have two wonderful sons. Aniskha earned a bachelor's degree in accounting and is an accountant by profession but a baseball mom at heart. God is the center of her life and her desire is to live the abundant life He intended for her.

Connect with Aniskha
Facebook: heavenlybutterfly242
Email: heavenlyfreebutterfly@gmail.com

For ordering information contact
the author at the email address above.

www.ingramcontent.com/pod-product-compliance
Lightning Source LLC
LaVergne TN
LVHW051501070426
835507LV00022B/2872